A Field Guide to
Actor Training

A Field Guide to

Actor Training

Navigating Acting Methods, Studio Classes,
Private Training, and Graduate and
Undergraduate Programs

Laura Wayth

An Imprint of Hal Leonard Corporation

Published in 2014 by Applause Theatre & Cinema Books
An Imprint of Hal Leonard Corporation
7777 West Bluemound Road
Milwaukee, WI 53213

Trade Book Division Editorial Offices
33 Plymouth St., Montclair, NJ 07042

Printed in the United States of America

Book design by Michael Kellner

Library of Congress Cataloging-in-Publication Data

Wayth, Laura.
A field guide to actor training / Laura Wayth.
pages cm
Includes bibliographical references and index.
ISBN 978-0-87910-824-3 (pbk.)
1. Acting--Study and teaching. I. Title.
PN2075.W39 2014
792.02'8--dc23
2014008324

www.applausebooks.com

To my mentors, Bruce Miller and Jeannie Woods

contents

acknowledgments

Special thanks to Professor Terry Hardcastle, University of Pittsburgh Department of Theatre Arts, for contributing the chapter on Lee Strasberg and the Method.

Special thanks also to Daniela Quinones and Shannon Ouellette for research assistance and to Dr. Larry Eilenberg, San Francisco State University, for his support.

Thanks also to my helpful and supportive editors at Hal Leonard Performing Arts Publishing Group, and to my many acting and teaching colleagues for offering their insights and perspectives.

Thanks to my mom and dad, who have always supported my dreams and education.

introduction

I had to learn everything the hard way. This book is my gift to you so that you don't have to.

I always knew that I wanted to be an actor. I tried, for a brief period of time, to pretend that I was interested in going to law school or having some sort of a "normal" profession. I tried different things: a brief stint in management consulting, a job as a freelance copywriter, and a series of jobs in academic administration. As nice as some of these jobs were, I was acutely aware, deep in the core of my being, that something was missing. I had this undeniable pull to something else. I knew in my heart and in my soul that I had no choice but to be an actor. Finally, I stopped fighting that truth and accepted it; I was, and would always be, an actor.

But my path remained terribly unclear. There was a fairly known and accepted route to other careers. If you wanted to be a doctor, you went to medical school; if you wanted to be an accountant, you went to business school; if you wanted to be a lawyer, you went to law school. But if you wanted to be an actor, you faced a lot of questions. Should you get training? How important *is* training? Where do you go to get training? What is the right kind of training?

And for me, although there was emotional support in abundance, there was no one to ask; there was no informed mentor in this area, no wise teacher. I was on my own, to forge my own path and to have my own successes and failures.

So I made a whole lot of mistakes, and really expensive ones to boot. I went to study at a graduate program that was not the right match for me, incurring $20,000 in student loan debt. I paid for private classes in New York that did not resonate with me. I didn't know good training from bad. I didn't know what kind of training I needed, or even whether I should continue my training. I plain old didn't know what I was looking for.

After much struggle, my story had a happy ending. Eventually, I found the kind of training that worked for me. Along the way, I got kicked around, inspired, knocked down, lifted up, and ultimately, I learned a heck of a lot the hard way.

Now I am a theatre professor and my happy ending is actually my happy beginning. I say this because a large part of my job is to help other people with their beginnings. Nearly every week, students come to my office, sit in my chair with the big leopard pillows, eat Hershey's miniatures out of the red bowl on my desk, and ask me the dreaded question: Should I be an actor? The ones who know that they have no choice but to be actors ask the other questions: Should I go to graduate school? Which graduate school should I go to? Should I seek out private training? Or should I just go out there and "do it"?

My job, in this book, is to try to help you to figure it out. I am going to help you to ask these questions of yourself, and I'm going to prepare you to make informed decisions as you try to carve your path. I am going to tell you what kinds of training are out there so that you can ask yourself the question: Is this training right for *me?*

This is the book that I wish I had had when I began my journey. It didn't exist. So I am writing it for you.

§

A note: You will observe that I always use the word "actor" in this book, regardless of whether I am speaking about a male person upon the stage or a female person upon the stage.

I never refer to myself as an "actress," or to my female students or colleagues as "actresses." To me, respect for the craft of acting dictates that all who practice it be termed "actors."

While the word "actress" is a common and accepted usage, to my way of thinking it undermines our true nature as artists. Other crafts, disciplines, and trades do not distinguish between genders: there are no "plumbesses," only plumbers; no "pilotesses," only pilots.

Being an actor is a craft. All who practice the craft of acting are actors.

1

The Big Questions

Should I Be an Actor?

No.

Let me explain.

If you have to ask the question, then the answer is no.

Whenever a student comes to my office and asks me the question "Should I be an actor?" I always say, "No." After I say it, they always make a face that looks like I just stepped on their pet gerbil. But this is the only truth. If you pose this question to me, it implies that there are other things that you can conceive of doing with your life and with your career. If you have other alternatives and other options—if there is anything else that you feel passionate about, or another interest you'd like to explore, you really should do it instead. "If you can do anything else, please, by all means, do it" were the discouraging, yet very wise words spoken to me on my first day of graduate school. It is the truth.

The only reason to be an actor is that you absolutely, truly cannot focus on any other pursuit. Only become an actor if you have made a real effort to commit to another path, and you just plain old *can't* do anything else. If you can conceive of yourself being happy by following another route, please strongly consider it. Becoming an actor is a wholehearted commitment and sacrifice. It is a commitment because you must invest every fiber of your being in this choice of profession; it is a sacrifice because in order to make

1

that kind of a commitment there is much in life that you have to be prepared to give up.

COMMITMENT AND SACRIFICE

To be an actor, you must have an unwavering belief in your craft and a passion for the work that makes everything else in life secondary.

An actor must be prepared not to live a normal life. I know that no one has a normal life these days, but the life of an actor is particularly abnormal. What do I mean by this? Creatures of all kinds seem to crave stability and predictability. My cat Sammy likes to know that breakfast will be served at nine and dinner will be served at five and nap time and window-sitting time comes in the middle. People have greater flexibility than this, of course, but in some small ways we are all like cats; we do best and we feel most secure and grounded when we have stability and routine.

As an actor, it will be up to you to create structure in your life. While many professions provide you with the stability of a routine, as an actor you must create these things for yourself. For actors, stability comes and goes with each new job. When you are employed, you'll spend much of your time lining up your next job. While you are auditioning, or even when you have acting work, you may need to patch together various jobs to make ends meet. You may find yourself temping on night shifts in offices, bartending at strange hours, or doing other work that you don't feel well suited to or stimulated by. You may find that you have just settled into a great apartment when you book a contract for a few months and have to sublet. You may love time on tour, or you may crave being at home, making spaghetti in your own kitchen and going to sleep in your own bed. You may have to miss your best friend's wedding because you have a show/audition/tech on the day of the ceremony. The list of possibilities goes on and on.

However the challenges manifest themselves for you, the important thing to realize is that becoming an actor is a step of the greatest commitment. You must not only be committed to your craft as a serious artist—constantly training to make yourself a better and better artist—but you must commit to the life of an actor itself. That life will become a priority over all other parts of life. It will often need to come before family and friends and security and comfort. Ask yourself now: What are the most important things in your life? Ask yourself what you are willing, and not willing, to have come second.

BEING AN ACTOR: A REALISTIC PICTURE

If you decide to face those challenges and make those sacrifices, you must also realize and acknowledge that, while good things can happen in this business, it is also a heartbreakingly difficult profession. This is not meant to be in any way discouraging. People can make their lives as actors and be happy. I am overjoyed every day to see many of my former students and colleagues working as actors and having fulfilling experiences. But before entering the business or deciding to train in this profession, we need to speak frankly about the day-to-day reality of being an actor.

It's much harder than you think.

Many times people tried to tell me what a rough road this profession is and I did not believe it. "It is hard for other people, but it will be different for me," I said to myself as a young actor. Many of my students say this to themselves, too, and I recognize my younger self in them. I was told, and my students are told, the odds of working steadily in this profession. They are warned, as I was warned, of the difficulties ahead, and yet they believe so unflinchingly in their talent and in their passion, as I believed in mine, that they decide to forge ahead anyway. That is wonderful. The world needs artists. But let's talk a little more before we go on so that you can be sure that you are asking yourself all of the right questions.

We may need to redefine your idea of being an actor. You may have a good and realistic sense of things, or, like many people, you may have an idea of what it might look like to be an actor that is very different from its reality. Movies and television shows *about* the profession can lead you to believe that it is glamorous and exciting, and you may have that kind of romanticized picture in your head. Being an actor can be glamorous and exciting from time to time, but it usually isn't. Being an actor is a job. Can that job be thrilling and exciting and fulfilling and creative and wonderful? Absolutely. But, like any job, it has its ups and downs, and for many it will have more downs than ups.

I entered the profession with an over-glamorized picture of backstage dressing rooms and opening nights, of Broadway marquees and two-character plays in funky Off-Off Broadway spaces. Because I wasn't dreaming of movies and fame like many young actors, I thought my vision was grounded and realistic and I praised myself for my practicality. The truth is I was still very far off base. The reality of being an actor can sometimes look a little more like this: "Why am I standing in Times Square wearing a giant Dalmatian suit and handing out flyers?"

I wish that I could tell you that this was the stuff of fiction. Alas, no: I've been the one in the Dalmatian suit, and I was there because I needed to pay rent. I had been auditioning steadily in New York, but I hit a dry spell. One hot August day I found myself on a promotion for a pet company, handing out flyers in front of the TKTS booth and scratching my head with my big Dalmatian paw, wondering how I'd gotten here. I came to New York to be an actor, not to impersonate a canine in sweltering heat.

Years later, one of the most talented people that I went to graduate school with, a woman who had worked consistently in wonderful theatres in leading roles, posted a picture of herself on Facebook wearing a bear costume in a similar location. I hurt for her and yet felt strangely vindicated at the same time. Her talent, her success, and her unfortunate bear suit all served as confirmation that actors, even the most talented and accomplished ones, often must often endure these sorts of indignities. A friend who had a stream of successful Broadway gigs found himself waiting tables again after the last show closed. A woman I knew who had played a major role in *Les Misérables* on Broadway found herself grateful years later to have a one-week engagement at a small equity theatre in the suburbs. This is the reality for most.

I entered the profession with an idealized view of what it would be like and found that, while there were wonderful, magical, satisfying moments, there were also many moments of the bear suit / Dalmatian suit / children's-theatre-tour-playing-a-stepsister-in-Cinderella variety. These were the moments when I found myself doing things to make a living that bore no resemblance to the craft that I was pursuing. This discrepancy between the profession that you picture and the day-to-day reality can challenge your belief in yourself, in your integrity, and in the integrity of the profession.

THE IMPORTANCE OF SELF-FAITH

We've seen that it can be challenging to sustain your faith in the profession, but let's talk a little more about an even more critical kind of faith. We have definitions for that word, usually tied to things spiritual and religious, but here I am going to use the term "self-faith." I use it to mean a belief in yourself that cannot be permanently shaken. Of course, we all have bad days and days where we feel dragged out or down on ourselves. In any part of life and in any profession there are those kinds of days, but being an actor is taxing to self in a way that nothing else is.

Why do I say this? All art is subjective. All art is subject to criticism. But unlike being a painter or a sculptor, where you may pour yourself into the art that you create, but maintain a physical separation between you and your creation, as a performer you *are* your art. And when you are your art, someone else's "rejection" of the art often feels like a rejection of you as a person. This feeling does not reflect the truth. As an actor, while you may be an artist and an individual, in the business sense of this world, you are actually a commodity.

If I am making minestrone soup and go to the store to shop for the ingredients that I need to make the soup, I may see the world's most amazing avocado at the store, but if I don't need an avocado to make the soup, I'm not going to buy one. I am going to keep looking and hope that I find a nice eggplant or zucchini or something that I really need to make the recipe. As an actor, my friend, you very often are the avocado. You may be talented and wonderful and perfect, but if you are not what is needed and required in that moment, if they need an eggplant and you are an avocado, no one will buy you. It doesn't matter how splendid an avocado you are. At other times you might find that when they do need an avocado, there is an even bigger, greener, darker, or riper avocado who would be even better for the recipe than you. I know you are not an avocado. Sometimes it would be easier if you were one. What I am saying is that it is rarely about you, and yet it almost always feels like it is about you. So, if you are to be an actor, you have to have an incredibly strong sense of self, and will have to grow to find ways to separate what you do and what you have to sell from who you are.

My graduate colleague Jason Pugatch wrote a very honest and direct book about the trials of working as an actor (2006). He says:

> You will face more rejection than you ever thought possible. Even the most successful actor is told no more times than yes. That's the lucky actor, because at least he's told something. Most are told nothing at all. The audition occurs, you take the elevator down to the lobby, step back onto Eighth Avenue, and go on with your life. The four-minute audition, which you spent hours preparing for, floats off into the great abyss of performances lost and jobs gone to another. This happens, at least in my case, ninety-five percent of the time.
>
> You'll never get used to it, but you can try. Certainly, you need to come to some understanding within yourself. This entails unraveling the confusion between your self-worth and your acting worth, because the two are entirely unrelated, though they feel at times inseparable. . . . But it never stops being painful.

I will never forget the day when a casting director from New York came into a musical theatre master class at the university where I was teaching. It was a room full of thirty-plus eager undergraduate BFA students, sheet music binders in hand, ready to work and to wow. The first thing that the casting director did, after the impressive recitation of his casting bio, was get up in front of the room, survey the students before him intently, and then make this bold and shocking statement.

"None of you are going to make it."

A hush fell over the room. People held their breath. A sense of panic set in. All of the students were wide-eyed and speechless and shocked.

Finally, one lone voice from the back of the room broke the silence.

"Screw you!" it said.

The casting director looked intently at the source of the voice, furrowed his brow, shifted his weight back and forth on his shiny loafers, examined his cuticles, and then reconsidered his position for a moment.

"Okay. *You* might."

Why do I tell you this story?

Is it to encourage you to disrespect industry professionals and fire expletives at those in power (actually, the student said something far more colorful than "screw you" . . . but you probably guessed that)?

No. I tell you this story because *this* is the kind of person who is equipped to be an actor.

The kind of person who has a prayer of making it as an actor is the person who will not be told "no," will not be affected by "no," will not accept "no," and will not take "no" on board. The kind of person bred for success and sanity in this profession is the person who will hear "no" and keep on moving and moving and moving through things, undaunted and determined, until he finally gets a "yes."

I am not this person.

Being an actor is hard for me. I take things personally. Even with all I know about this business, I cannot separate my craft from myself. To criticize my craft as an actor or singer is to criticize me in my mind. Although intellectually I know the ins and outs of the profession, I still have not achieved the ability to separate my professional self from my personal self. I need people to like me. I need people to accept me and approve of me. I like it when people praise me. I love being an actor, and I'm a good actor. But given my emotional makeup, given my need for stability and security and a routine home life, the profession is a difficult fit for me. I still am and always will be an actor, but I have moved more from being a practicing actor in the middle of the profession to being an academic who acts part-time and spends the rest of her time training other actors. I train those who *do* have the right temperament to make a success of it, and their success is my success. I am happy and whole. As a full-time professional actor, I was not.

In short, to be an actor you have to have such an unrelenting faith in yourself and in your talent that no one can knock you down—permanently, anyway. I like to think of this kind of person as having the power to become something like the Terminator. Remember the movie *Terminator 2?* No matter how much people try to knock the Terminator down and dismantle it, its liquid metal body re-congeals and it comes back stronger and more powerful than ever.

That's the kind of toughness I would wish for anyone embarking on a career as an actor—the kind that only increases when you get knocked around. At the same time, I know only too well that acting attracts people who are unusually sensitive, feeling, open, and vulnerable—people who aren't likely to have the thick skin they need to survive in the profession. I believe that a thick skin *can* be grown and developed; it's a skill that can be learned. But for certain personalities it is exceptionally difficult. For me, it was an enormous challenge and one that I never truly overcame. Ask yourself: are you more like me, or more like the kid in the BFA program who stood up to the casting director, or are you somewhere in the middle? Be honest with yourself and know who you are. There is no shame in being whomever and whatever kind of person you are. I only ask that you take a good, hard look at your true nature and your emotional makeup before you make the decision to enter this profession.

THE ODDS

In the movie *Star Wars,* when Han Solo, in an effort to outrun enemy fighters, dares to navigate his decrepit ship, the Millennium Falcon, through an asteroid belt, the robot C3PO tells him, "Sir, the possibility of successfully navigating an asteroid field is approximately 3,720 to 1."

Han Solo replies, "Never tell me the *odds*."

If you know the movie, you know that Han successfully beats those odds and moves his ship successfully through the many perils of the asteroid field. You too might beat the odds of the acting business and might, like Han Solo, want to say to me, "Never tell me the odds."

I do think that you absolutely must understand the odds of the game that you are playing if this is the game that you choose to play.

As of the writing of this book, the Actor's Equity Association, the union of professional stage actors, reports a 90 percent unemployment rate for its members. This is truly horrifying. This means that only 10 percent of professional actors are employed as actors at any given time. Even when you are fortunate enough to be employed, the salary is usually not sufficient to sustain you well, especially given the cost of living in a city like New York.

BUT WHAT ABOUT LUCK?

As with everything in life, in acting there is room for luck. There is such a phenomenon as being in the right place at the right time with the right people. If you have the "right stuff"—the right look, the right talent, the right type, and real craft—the stars may come together in your favor.

It happens. It has happened for many of my students and fellow actors. It hasn't happened for some of my most talented students and fellow actors. A success in this business is that very fortunate cocktail of talent, opportunity, and timing. And it does happen. Sometimes.

WHAT ELSE CAN I DO?

Many times when students come to me with the question "Should I be an actor," I try to get them to think about any other possibilities within the world of theatre. The profession is overcrowded with actors, and while no career path or training is without its challenges and difficulties, there are other ways to make a career in theatre besides becoming an actor. More than another greatly talented actor, the profession may need another greatly talented lighting designer, costume designer, scenic designer, stage manager, or technical director. Think about other possibilities within the world of the theatre. It takes far more talent than the talent of actors to realize a great piece of theatre. You may have talents and passions within this world that you have yet to discover. If you think that you might, get as much exposure to these other areas as possible. Go and speak to faculty and staff at universities or local theatres who are doing these kinds of jobs. Ask them about their part of the profession. Ask them about how they trained and about their struggles and opportunities. See if you can assist them and learn from them (everyone loves free help)! You may find that many of them started out as actors themselves and along the way discovered another path that spoke to them equally where their talents were more nurtured and rewarded.

THE DECISION TO BE AN ACTOR

If you have carefully thought about all that I have presented to you about the reality of being an actor, if you have asked yourself all of the necessary questions about your life priorities and your personal makeup, and you still have reached the informed decision that, yes, this is in fact what you want to do with your career and your life, our next step is to figure out how. While there are many books written about how to shape a career in the acting business that touch on such topics as how to audition and how to be a player in the business world of being an actor, in our conversation together, we will focus on the first and foundational step, training.

2

Why Actor Training
Is Important

Should I Get Further Training?

The next question that I get most often from students after "Should I be an actor?" is "Should I go to a school and get more training in acting, or should I just go out there and 'do it?'"

If you've decided to read *A Field Guide to Actor Training*, you can probably anticipate my answer. While there are many paths to becoming an actor, I am a firm believer in the value of training. Most people understand that they won't be hired as a ballerina or a concert pianist without years and years of daily study and struggle; for some reason, though, people seem to believe that they can just "go out and become" an actor. Like music and dance, acting is an art form that is developed by training and disciplining the mind and the body.

I believe that to play roles that demand great artistry, one must absolutely get as much training as possible. I can think of no greater acting challenge than that of playing Hamlet—and I would never tell an actor, no matter how innately gifted and talented, that he could be Hamlet without years of training and discipline. The physical, mental, and emotional stamina demanded by this most difficult role, and the crucial facility with textual and poetic analysis, require years of developing and refining one's craft. Similarly, I would not want a Yelena who was not thoroughly trained in voice and speech, physical disciplines, and the craft of acting to be in my production of Chekhov's *Uncle Vanya.* Such nuanced works of literary art demand individuals who have thoroughly cultivated their own artistry through training. To really come into your own fully as an artist requires as much study as possible.

That said, there are other schools of thought on this. I would say that most people coming from an academic perspective, as I am, will tell you the same thing: that you must seek out rigorous training before entering the profession. You must remember that we academics see acting, by virtue of where we have placed ourselves in our professions, more as an art form than as a business.

But there are those with a different perspective. I believe that the great majority of people working as casting directors and other industry professionals might tell you something different. The prevailing belief when I was in the industry years ago was that graduate training may or may not be useful; it is your experience within the profession that counts. I remember a New York casting director telling me that graduate study was a waste of time and really didn't matter "unless you go to Yale or NYU" (two top training programs at the time that casting people got excited about). While not all industry professionals necessarily agree, I do think that oftentimes they share a particular vantage point. Casting directors may often be looking more at who is a fit for a given role, based on a look or a quality, than at an actor's proficiency as an artist. They will look for a successful track record of working in reputable theatres and may not consider the quality of an actor's training.

Let's suppose for a minute that you are about to graduate with a BA (Bachelor of Arts) or BFA (Bachelor of Fine Arts) degree and are trying to figure out your next step as an actor. First, we have to acknowledge that there are many different types of BFA programs. A really strong one has probably prepared you to enter the profession just as well as a good graduate program can. A lesser program may not have given you all of the craft tools that you need, so it will help to supplement what you know with a graduate program or studio course work in areas of weakness.

It is difficult to truly assess where your training and education may have holes. One of the ways to begin to gain an idea of areas in your craft that may need strengthening is to do as much theatre as possible. It is when we are working in theatre, rather than studying it, that we begin to see our strengths and weaknesses clearly. This does not mean that the work needs to be at a professional level—simply doing the work in a performance arena, rather than in an academic environment, may help you to see where you are comfortable and confident and where you are not.

For the sake of our discussion, let us suppose that you either attended a BFA program that was lacking in some way or that you simply have a BA degree. If you were to ask me, "Should I go to graduate school or a certificate program, or should I just go for it and go directly to New York," here is what I would ask you:

"What can you sell that other people can't easily sell? Is there something that you have that is rare and hard to come by?"
In my ten years of teaching, the only two students whom I encouraged to enter the profession directly from a BA program without additional training programs were these students:

- A pretty girl of average height and weight who was a true triple threat. That is, she sang and danced and acted equally well. She was uniquely gifted in all three areas.
- An incredibly handsome African American male with a booming voice who sang and tap-danced.

Why these students? They had something unique and rare to offer. The guy had a unique look and skill set. The girl was equally proficient in three areas. Had any ingredient been missing in either one of these students, I would have encouraged them to seek additional formal training programs first. They had a rare combination of ingredients that made them standouts and made them highly employable, meaning that the odds of success were somewhat increased for them given what they had to offer the industry. While it was no guarantee of success, they had a shot.

Even when I do recommend jumping straight into the fray of trying to make a living as an actor, it's anything but a license to stop learning. As an actor, your education is never finished. Every day I learn something new about acting. I face a problem that is difficult to solve, I hit a roadblock that needs a new tool, or I am exposed to a new idea or a new way of thinking. To be an actor is to constantly challenge yourself. The actor who stops training is the actor who stagnates and perpetually draws from his or her limited bag of tricks. Those actors get stale and boring fast. True craftspeople in the profession are constantly challenging themselves and finding new ways to grow.

There are all kinds of ways to train and continue your education as an actor. As an academic, my go-to answer is "Seek a formal training program," but this is only one path. Many of my actor friends who work consistently in the industry did *not* go to degree-granting or certificate-granting training programs. These actors took classes and accessed different modes of training to supplement craft areas that they felt needed to be strengthened. Different paths work for different people. The most important thing truly is not necessarily *how* and in what form you work on your craft as an actor, but that you *are* constantly working on it and growing.

At the end of this book, I will try to answer some questions that actors like you may ask. For now, let's look at some different types of training so that you have an idea of what options may be out there for you.

KINDS OF PRIVATE TRAINING

Studios

Acting studios are designed to give actors more training, but they are not degree-granting programs. Rather, you take individual classes that interest you. Studio classes are a wonderful way to learn specific techniques—often from highly qualified teachers who are experienced actors. They can also be a terrific way to meet other actors and to gain a sense of community, especially if you are new in a city.

One of the best places to find acting studios (if you live in New York or L.A.) is the actor's trade paper, *Backstage*, now online at www.backstage.

com (look at the resources section on their website). Here you will find a list of acting schools organized by category and listed alphabetically. You will be able to find descriptions of classes, the training level that they are intended for (beginning, intermediate, advanced), and the type of training provided. Some studios are far better than others. While there can be training gems in unexpected places (training, after all, is really only as good or bad as the individual instructor and the students present), it may be a good start to look for programs that have a substantial history. The Stella Adler Studio of Acting and the William Esper Studio, for example, are long-established schools that might be a good place to start your search (at the end of this book I will list some programs like this for you to check out). Word of mouth is your best bet. Talk to actors and find out training that they have found valuable. A wonderful place (if you are a New York actor) to get the inside scoop is a trip to the Drama Book Shop. Go and talk to the people working there. Chances are the person stocking the shelves is an actor with some valuable information who can tell you what is around. Actors like to talk about acting.

One caveat. Some studios will offer classes with industry professionals, especially casting directors. These training classes can be absolutely wonderful if you take them for the right reasons. Casting directors teaching classes can give you practical and concrete information from their perspective. The ability to see your work through the lens of someone in the trenches of your industry can be enormously helpful. This is a great reason to take these kinds of classes. If your primary motivation in taking these classes is to connect with casting people in the hopes of being cast, I would urge you to reshuffle your priorities. Although occasionally this does happen, this is not the best reason for seeking out this kind of training. These classes can be costly, and many a hungry actor has eaten his share of ramen noodles for a month ponying up the money to be "seen" by industry personnel in this environment. Train for the sake of training and think of any industry connections that you may make as a wonderful added bonus, but not the primary motivation.

Certificate Programs

Certificate programs are exactly what they sound like. At the end of training in these programs you are offered a certificate of completion rather than a master's degree in acting.

Certificate programs can be wonderful training grounds. Again, training is as valuable or not valuable as the instructor teaching the classes and the student community taking the classes; and many programs offer great coursework with very inspiring teachers. Certificate programs also frequently require a commitment of time and money that is nearly equal to what you would spend to attend an MFA program. If you are prepared to invest that time and money, you might consider looking for an MFA degree-granting program. Why? For one simple reason: the MFA is the standard and recognized terminal degree in the field of theatre. One cannot teach acting at a college or university coming out of a certificate program in most cases. If you know for a fact that you will never, ever, ever be interested in teaching, and if your only interest is growth in your craft, a certificate training program may very well be for you. But if you want to leave options open for your future and make an investment, not only in your growth and craft as an actor, but in your education in the eyes of the world, there is value in a traditional and recognized educational model. Really look at the individual program; in some rare cases both a certificate *and* a master's degree may be offered. As you construct your career, it may be wise to think about maximizing your options for the future.

If you do decide that a certificate training program meets your needs, look at this website: http://theaterschools.findthebest.com. Select the "certificate" option under "acting degrees offered."

It is always wise, too, to ask industry personnel what their perception is of a given training program. A one-night business workshop with an agent, manager, or casting director at an acting studio might provide you Q&A time to ask for an opinion. Knowing the industry's perception of training programs, as well as other actors' perceptions, is always a great move.

Coaching

An acting coach is an experienced actor, director, or acting teacher who works with actors, usually in a one-on-one capacity, to address that actor's specific training or performance needs. Many coaches specialize in audition coaching; that is, you, the actor, bring them the tired monologue that you have been taking to auditions (most likely without huge success) and they help you to see the strengths and weaknesses of your chosen material or your approach to the work. A good coach can offer an outside perspective to help you to shape your audition, or perhaps suggest audition material that may serve you better

Coaches can do far more than prepare you for auditions. A skilled acting coach can also assist you with specific techniques, usually as those techniques relate to a given project that you are working on. Let's say that there is a role that is a real stretch for you, and you just can't find a way into the work. A skilled coach can help you to find tools that will support you in approaching the role and solving problematic moments in the script. The benefit of coaching is that it addresses your specific and immediate craft needs. Because coaching does not usually provide the actor with a specific, methodical training system or way of working, but is a way of addressing specific challenges, it is a good supplement to training but not a substitution for it.

In addition to acting coaches, you can find coaches to assist you with other areas of training and performance, such as

- Voice and speech coaching, including assistance with dialects, vocal support, and standardization of speech (particularly helpful if you have a strong home dialect)
- Physical acting coaching including one-on-one training in physical disciplines like Laban and Alexander Technique
- Musical theatre coaching, including coaching on song style and delivery, song selection, and musical storytelling
- Classical text coaching (a subdivision of acting coaching),

i.e., assistance with the specific demands of acting
Shakespeare and heightened texts

Beware! There are all kinds of coaches. I've had terrific ones and I've had dreadful ones. Anyone can call themselves a coach. The best way to find a good one is word of mouth. Talk to other actors. Who do they recommend? If you have a network of graduates from your university who are working in the profession, ask them. Talk to local theatres. Call up theatre departments and acting schools and ask if they have recommendations. The theatre world is a small place and someone will know someone. *Backstage*, the actor's trade paper (now online), also has a list of coaches. Don't be afraid to check out a potential acting coach's background. Look at their resume. Ask them how they trained and what techniques they teach (their answer will probably make more sense to you after reading the rest of this book). Be clear on the price, and compare rates by consulting with other actors. Schedule a first meeting and be certain that you have a rapport and that you are comfortable with them as a person. No matter what kind of training you are seeking and no matter how experienced or inexperienced you are, a good coach is always a great move.

SHOULD I GO TO GRADUATE SCHOOL?

As I stated previously, I am a firm believer in the value of training. One of the best ways to train as in actor, in my opinion, is to take concentrated time that is strictly devoted to the study of your craft. It is certainly not the only way. You do not need an MFA to be an actor. Time spent training outside of a formal program can be equally valuable. What I *like* about graduate training is that attending graduate school for acting gives you the time and space required to develop as an artist.

A visual artist friend of mine once described his time spent obtaining a three-year MFA in photography as a "gift." "What other time would I be allowed to put everything else in my life on hold and focus only on making art?" he once said to me. This is the true beauty of time spent in a graduate program for acting: it provides a framework for you to focus exclusively on developing your craft and artistry.

A strong graduate training program in acting, in my opinion, is one that has an equal blend and balance of the following areas:

- Training in voice and speech
- Training in movement disciplines
- Substantive studio acting time, offering training in classical and contemporary acting with individualized attention from instructors
- Substantial opportunities for hands-on learning through production opportunities
- A grounding in the discipline from a historical and theoretical perspective

To my mind, these are the primary ingredients of a quality graduate training experience. While the methods and style of training will vary greatly from program to program, this is the basic framework of what you should be looking for in a graduate school. Be certain to look for a program with balance; too little time and focus in any of these areas will leave gaps in your training. Voice and movement training, for example, are as integral to actor training as studio acting training. A program that offers too little hands-on time with its voice or movement faculty may not enable you to develop as fully as you might in another program. The opposite can also be true; is there an equal balance of acting classes? Is the program so movement, voice, or theory-based that there is not enough studio acting time? Are there not enough opportunities for learning and training through performance? A good program is made up equally of all of these areas.

I cannot stress enough the value of individualized training. Beware of the too-large training program! I attended such a program for a very brief time in New York years ago. I remember finding it odd that what I thought was a highly selective program had ninety students in its first-year graduate acting class. I remember walking into my first day of graduate orientation in an enormous auditorium filled with a sea of incoming actors and being slightly bewildered. These kinds of programs are what I call "cash cow" programs. They draw students with the prestige of their name or location, charge substantial tuition, and are far too large in scale to give students the kind of training needed. That said, there are nuggets of wonderfulness in any training experience, and my brief graduate stint at this program with my eighty-nine fellow actors was no exception. Still, this model is in no way an ideal training environment. Try to find a program where you are not one of many. The real world of acting is competitive and overstuffed enough. Graduate training is your time to be nurtured and developed.

I believe that an ideal training program has somewhere between ten and twenty actors in a class at any given time. It's a little bit like Goldilocks and the three bears (you know, "This porridge is too hot, this porridge is too cold, this porridge is just right . . ."). If it is too small a training program with too few fellow graduate actors, there will not be enough variety and diversity in the ensemble experience. If it is too large a graduate acting class, there will not be enough performance opportunity and not enough attention to your individual needs and development. A training class with ten to twenty actors is a perfect size to foster an enriching ensemble experience and personalized attention.

How Do I Find a Graduate Training Program?

While one can look at individual universities and their graduate theatre training programs and inquire directly with the program about audition procedures, one of the most cost-effective and time-effective way of seeking out graduate training opportunities is by attending the national unified auditions. URTA, the University/Resident Theatre Association (www.urta.com), holds annual unified auditions and interviews every winter in three separate locations: New York City, Chicago, and San Francisco. Actors wishing to attend graduate programs have the opportunity to audition for many university graduate training programs. While the URTA unified auditions have a screening process and, not all of the actors who attend the conference will necessarily be seen by URTA's member schools, non-URTA schools also attend this annual conference to search for interested students. There are some wonderful programs out there that are not necessarily URTA member schools.

To Pay or Not to Pay, That Is the Question

Graduate training comes roughly in two categories: the kind of training that you pay for and the kind of training that you, well, sort of don't. I qualify the second kind because, just like there is no such thing as a free puppy (a puppy needs puppy chow, flea meds, neutering, and a chew toy), there is no such thing as a free education. A "free" graduate education can cost a little more than you think, and there are all kinds of costs to be considered and factored in, not all of them monetary.

We'll talk about the programs that you pay for soon, but for now let's talk a little more about a "free ride." There are many programs out there, from the very wonderful to the not–so-wonderful, and everything in between, that will in essence "pay you" to go to graduate school. These programs audition graduate actors on a set cycle (say every year, every two years, or every three years) and make offers to a select group of students. These chosen students are offered an educational package that usually consists of a full tuition waiver and a graduate stipend. Graduate stipends are usually given in exchange for some sort of a service to the program. This could be a stipend given for teaching an introductory acting course or other course in the department's undergraduate programs each semester, or could come from working in the program's scene shop, costume shop, box office, or administrative offices. The particular terms will vary, but an actor offered this package will be providing some sort of service to the department.

A stipendiary position in a graduate training program can have some real advantages. The reality is that a working actor does not command a large salary and an actor's financial picture is usually a little precarious at best. Avoiding taking out costly educational loans for graduate training in acting can be a smart move. Leaving graduate school with only a small amount of educational or personal debt is a much more relaxed way to enter or re-enter your professional life as an actor. Also, working another job outside of a graduate program in acting is a near impossibility, because of the program's demands on your time. It is nice to have your "job" (your stipendiary position) be a part of your training.

That said, you do need to be aware that often these "free rides," while financially a much better deal than a non-stipendiary position, may still have costs. Graduate assistantships, while they can defray your living expenses, generally are not quite enough to live on. It is conceivable that you will still need to dip into personal savings or take out some additional loans during the course of your training. While tuition costs are covered, be aware that there may also be some student fees of which you are not aware. Before you accept a stipend and tuition waiver package to attend graduate school, be certain that you carefully look at the specific costs involved in attending the program and make a realistic assessment of the cost of living in the area where you will be going to school. It may in fact be a great deal, but you need to have all of your facts up front.

Also be aware that there are more ways to pay for a program than financially. There are many schools where the services provided by the acting student in exchange for the stipend are quite fair, reasonable, and constructive. In an ideal stipendiary position, the work that you do for the program will actually be a valuable part of your education, such as learning to teach, learning to sew and hang lights, or learning to work in a box office. Oftentimes, however, sad as it is to say, a graduate actor can become slave labor for a program. I can think of a few training programs where the graduate assistants are nearly run into the ground with more assistantship hours than hours of actor training. In such programs, students often become exhausted and demoralized and do not have the energy to put into their training since so much of it is being diverted to working as an assistant. To avoid this, try to gain a realistic sense of the workload of the assistantship. No one can tell you this with greater accuracy than current students in the graduate program. Chances are that if the assistantship hours rival or exceed the training hours, the program may not serve you optimally.

In addition to paying financially and with your labor, there is a "payment" of time. An actor will generally spend two or three years in residence in a graduate training program, depending on its structure (there are some rare one-year programs, but generally those are certificate programs rather than MFA programs). Weighing your investment of time and emotional and intellectual resources is the hardest part of this decision. It is easy to determine the financial costs of attending a program, and it is relatively easy to assess the workload of a given assistantship, but the larger question, "Is attending this program worth the investment of my time?" is a tougher call.

Ask yourself this most important question: What is it that you hope to gain from attending this program? Every actor has different goals and the nature of your goals will undoubtedly dictate the best course of action to meet your specific needs. For example, my goal in attending graduate school was, ultimately, to teach, rather than to re-enter the profession as a full-time actor. In my particular case, the programs that were offering me "free rides" I knew would not have the kind of weight and credibility that would give me the best chance at future employment in teaching. For me, opting for the expensive program rather than the "free ride" was the best choice, as I knew that the program I attended would not only prepare me well for a career in teaching, but would have credibility to other academics once I hit the job market. For me, taking out a chunk of loans to attend a well-respected program was the right choice. Everyone's path is different. Take a good look at your specific goals. Look at what the program's graduates are doing. If your goal is to work as an actor, how are the program's alums doing? Where are they working? Is there a lone "success story" that this school is parading around, or are there many graduates of this program working consistently? If your goal is to teach, where have graduates of this program accepted teaching appointments? Know your goals and do your homework. Sometimes it is worth waiting for the right program. Do not simply go to the first program that will accept you because you want so badly to be an actor! Sometimes getting into the right graduate school can take a while. If you haven't been accepted into a program you feel is the right fit, work, audition, gain life experience and try again next year.

Is It a Fit?

It seems that most actors want to go to the big name graduate program. Forget the name. Does it fit?

You might go shopping and find a beautiful Versace dress for sale. Just because it's a Versace dress doesn't mean that it fits you. If you're five feet tall, that orange chiffon gown with the train isn't going to look as good on you as the $90 black cocktail dress from Bloomingdales. Don't be blinded by the name.

An impressive label doesn't guarantee an optimal learning environment. I can think of two top-tier graduate schools that I visited that I felt that I should love, and yet something about them didn't sit right with me. They felt aggressive and mismatched for me. When I found the program where I belonged, I walked into the lobby and it felt strangely like home. Trust your instincts! Don't look solely at name and reputation. These are important considerations, but these things will mean nothing if you cannot have a comfortable training environment that feels like it resonates with you as a person.

Every graduate program has a different culture and philosophy of actor training. Approaches to learning the craft of acting can be drastically different at any given program. In addition to visiting the school, also pay careful attention to what the department emphasizes about its training. Carefully read their website and compare it to the websites of other programs that you are considering. For instance, if the program description emphasizes a commitment to new works and theatre for social change, and this is not your primary passion, it may not be the right fit. Look at the program's department statement. Does it align with your own personal and professional mission?

When interviewing/auditioning for graduate schools, realize that you are interviewing *them* in return! This is an empowering way to think which can only make you more attractive to prospective schools; it will also help you to evaluate a program to see if it's a fit.

If you are invited to join a graduate program, do not accept the offer sight unseen. Go and visit the campus. Visit classes and see what they are like. Talk to current students. You will know by spending a day or even a few hours at a program if it has a chance of being right for you.

In the next sections of this book, we will look at different acting, voice, and physical training methodologies. Some programs train exclusively in one primary acting methodology, while others are a synthesis or mix of a few different approaches. Oftentimes the methods and approach to training at a given program will be shaped by the individuals on faculty and the training systems they were taught. We will break down and summarize these different approaches to training, so that *you* can find out what kind of training will be best for *you*! After all, you are your own artist.

3

Stanislavsky, the Foundation of It All

When we are on stage, we are in the here and now.—Konstantin Stanislavsky

There is no other way, to my mind, to begin our conversation about acting methodologies than with the work of Konstantin Stanislavsky. Stanislavsky, or Stanislavski (depending on who you are), is without a doubt the most important name in actor training.

Which is right, the "y" or the "i"? Neither! Both! Good old Konstantin (or Constantin) Stanslavski/y was a Russian, so he wrote his name using the Cyrillic alphabet: Станиславский. Depending on who is writing his name and when they are writing it, it can be Romanized (translated into the Latin alphabet) in different ways. I'm going to use the "y" spelling here because I think it is more elegant and appears to be the preferred spelling among most English-speaking scholars. But what is in a name, anyway? The important thing to know is that he is the father of modern acting practice and training. Stanislavsky's theories and ideas, in one form or another, will be a large part of your training as an actor. His principles—his way of thinking about acting and the creative process of being an actor—permeate our thinking and influence almost every other acting methodology and system of training out there today, whether he is credited or not. As Bella Merlin (2007) writes,

The study of his ideas is on almost every acting academy timetable, every drama degree syllabus, every theatre studies exam, and—be it implicitly or explicitly— his terms and theories are on the lips of most Western acting practitioners.

And yet, bizarrely, he's often dismissed. Why so? Is it due to poor translations? Misdirected editors? Vainglorious gurus who clamor to "claim" Him? Postmodern performers who consider psychology obsolete? Could it even be due to his own inability from time to time to express his emerging ideas succinctly, with the result that his writings sometimes seem to go round in circles and muddy his practical propositions?

Whatever the reason, his highly hands-on notions have frequently become distorted into something academic and atrophied. And let's face it, the alternatives are very attractive: David Mamet is muscular; Ivana Chubbuck is chic; Suzuki is sexy. Yet all of them use Stanislavsky, whether they know it or not.

Merlin hits the nail on the head. I remember as a graduate student feeling that I should read Stanislavsky's seminal works: *An Actor Prepares*, *Building a Character*, and *Creating a Role*. I am ashamed to say that I needed a "family-size" bag of M&M's to get me through a chapter of any of these works. I knew that I was reading some of the most important thoughts about acting that I would ever encounter—and yet I could not hang on to them, as hard as I tried. As I felt my eyes moving across each page, my brain was moving across something else entirely.

An Actor Prepares, the first in Stanislavsky's writings and his most famous book, is written in the form of the fictitious diary of the imaginary "Kostya," a young and passionate student of acting under a master teacher, Tortsov. Kostya is a wide-eyed newbie, and Tortsov sets his inexperienced and erroneous student's thinking right in a series of lessons. This book devotes itself to an exploration of the imaginative process of an actor and development of the actor's imaginative skills, while the subsequent book, *Building a Character*, deals with the physical creation of character on stage through vocal and physical choices (again with the guidance of the wise and philosophical teacher, Tortsov). The final book in Stanislavsky's trilogy, *Creating a Role*, delves into the creation of character by examining three widely contrasting plays: Griboyedov's *Woe from Wit*, Shakespeare's *Othello*, and Gogol's *The Inspector General*. *Creating a Role* looks at the process of studying the script, investigating the inner life of a role, and finding the physical shape and container of the role.

There is no doubt that these seminal works form the foundation for our modern acting craft and that their value should in no way be undermined or neglected. Still, I am not the only person to feel that there is something strangely inaccessible about them. Ms. Merlin's statement that Stanislavsky's very practical ideas often go around in circles resonates with my experience of them. Wonderful ideas, with a core of true elegant simplicity, are expressed so circuitously in the books that one has to work hard indeed to crack the outer shell of the nut to get to its meaty center. Much of this is no doubt imbedded in cultural difference and the time at which Stanislavsky was writing. And I suspect that Stanislavsky was further formulating and clarifying many of his ideas *as* he was writing these books, despite years of percolating them, and that in a way the struggling student Kostya was actually Stanislavsky attempting to formulate and articulate his own ideas and concepts. Still, although the works may *take* work to understand, Stanislavsky has most of the answers in these books that we, as actors, will ever need.

Who Was Stanislavsky?

As you know by now, he was a Russian. Stanislavsky lived from 1863 to 1938, and with Vladimir Nemirovich-Danchenko he founded the Moscow Art Theatre in 1897. At the time at which Stanislavsky began to work in theatre and to think about theatre, Russia, the international community, and the craft of acting needed him rather desperately. The style of theatre at the time was robotic and passionless. There was very little concern for truthful, realistic creation of character on stage. Acting was histrionic and one-dimensional. There began to be a kind of hunger for acting that was far more organic, passionate, and real than the customary offerings of the time.

This set the stage for the founding of the Moscow Art Theatre in 1897. Once founded, the Moscow Art Theatre became a kind of laboratory where Stanislavsky could investigate the mysteries of acting. The work that he did here would have far-reaching international effects as a more realistic and truthful approach to acting took root.

Particularly significant was the Moscow Art Theatre production of *The Seagull*, written by Anton Chekhov, in 1898. Praised for its realistic acting, *The Seagull* was a game changer for theatre, not only in Russia, but internationally. Chekhov's collaboration with the Moscow Art Theatre changed the way theatre was made, resulting in the creation of other classics including *Uncle Vanya*, *The Three Sisters*, and *The Cherry Orchard* (Merlin 2007). Here Stanislavsky broke away from the acting style of the time, successfully creating performances that had a greater sense of truth. It was there, at the Moscow Art Theatre, in collaboration with Anton Chekhov, that a revolution of realism in the theatre began.

Stanislavsky often confuses us and is misunderstood by us because, like every great thinker, his thinking was fluid rather than rigid. What do I mean by this? I mean that Stanislavsky, in response to his inner promptings and to the cultural, political, and scientific developments of his time, changed his ideas drastically during his career. At first his quest for a realistic theatre led him to a preoccupation with the nature of emotion. Later he recognized that his earlier ideas were flawed. Drawn to the concepts swirling around him in other fields, Stanislavsky veered away from his emphasis on emotion (namely a concept we'll discuss in more detail, called **emotional memory**) to focus primarily on action (what became known as the **method of physical actions**) (Merlin 2007). These two very different ways of thinking about theatre—one way driven primarily by emotional experience and the other driven primarily by physical action—sets the stage for a fracturing of Stanislavsky's ideas, most notably as they came to America (more on that later on in our section on Lee Strasberg and the Method). Stanislavsky's ideas from later on in his career seem drastically different from his initial ideas. To look at either set of thoughts without charting through his entire process is to oversimplify both and to understand neither.

Stanislavsky's Method?

This all raises the question, what exactly *is* Stanislavsky's "method"?

To answer that, we need to know this: Stanislavsky really didn't *want* to create a "method" or a "system." In fact, he out-and-out rejected this notion. He did not believe in creating a bible or a gospel that others would follow; rather he was a pioneer trying to understand truth in theatre. Were he alive today, no doubt he would continue reinvestigating and redefining his insights. Because Stanislavsky's thoughts were in motion, always undergoing reinvention, we must honor his thoughts as being fluid and in flux, approaching his work, not as a bible to be followed, but as a launching point to open up other ideas. I feel that it is very important to see Stanislavsky's work as a series of theatrical principles—a springboard for creativity rather than a defined and prescriptive system. Stanislavsky himself denied that there was a Stanislavsky system. He claimed, quite modestly, that the only authentic and indisputable system occurred in nature itself (Moore 1984).

Basic Principles

Any investigation of Stanislavsky means that we have to pay attention to two main areas: the psychological elements of character and the physical elements of the creation of character. Stanislavsky recognized that the physical reality and the psychological reality that the actor experiences needed to be addressed simultaneously. As he saw it, psychological reality and physical reality were dependent on and informed by one another.

EMOTIONAL MEMORY

This term is one hell of a leaden matzo ball sitting in the soup of the acting room!

The idea of emotional memory (or emotional recall, as it is sometimes called) is misunderstood, misrepresented, and has caused many a fight among actors. Pay attention to this term, as its interpretation and use in America has bitterly divided some of the greatest acting practitioners of all time. This term, investigated and coined by Stanislavsky, was interpreted and changed once it hit the United States, forming the foundation of the Method in America. We will talk about that more later on, but for now the important thing to realize is that Stanislavsky's method (inappropriate a term though that may be, since Stanislavsky himself, as we said, did not seek to create a method) and what has come to be known as *the* Method are, in fact, very different things, although they supposedly spring from the same origin.

But back to emotional memory. What *is* emotional memory, anyway?

Emotional memory is a tool developed by Stanislavsky to provide the actor with a way of having a genuine emotional experience as the character in a given moment in a play. The actor recalls an event that he or she has experienced in the past in order to recreate those feelings in the present, using them to play the emotion in a given scene. For example, if I am playing a role where I discover that my sister has been hit by a car, as the actor, I may try to recall the experience that I had when I was ten years old and my dog, Scout, was hit by a car in the middle of my suburban neighborhood. If I can remember with accuracy the events of the day that beloved Scout was discovered, after being hit by the blue Toyota in the street, and my shock and horror at the site of him, I can summon up those emotions and use them to play the scene with my sister and look as though I am having a similar realistic and truthful reaction.

So, emotional memory is exactly what it sounds like: remembering an emotion from the past in order to synthesize a similar emotional experience on stage in the present. The thinking goes that if the actor spends enough time in rehearsal and training using emotional memory, in the moment it is required onstage, the emotion needed will emerge as a conditioned reflex, much as the piano player practicing a difficult passage over and over again in rehearsal will have the muscle memory needed to sail through the passage in performance.

Although emotional memory was a foundational idea of Stanislavsky's, he later began to rework the idea. In the last five years of his work and life, Stanislavsky radically shifted his thinking about the craft of acting. He came to feel that the technique of emotional memory just put actors through the wringer, exhausting them and making them nervous, hysterical messes. Emotions, he recognized, were draining to genuinely reproduce onstage. So he began to look for other solutions.

Eventually Stanislavsky arrived at the notion that the body itself held the answer to recreating truthful emotional experience onstage. He began to see that the body was a more reliable theatrical tool than the intellect or the emotions; that is, it was far easier for the actor to replicate an experience using the body than his or her emotional or intellectual life, which were highly variable. Thus his method of physical actions was born, replacing emotional memory as the primary tool in his approach to acting.

METHOD OF PHYSICAL ACTIONS

Stanislavsky came to see the relationship between the actor's psyche and his or her physical life very clearly. This led him to the following notion: the actor did not need to delve deeply into a past emotional experience to recreate the appearance of an emotion on stage. Rather, emotion could be stimulated on stage through a series of physical actions.

Stanislavsky postulated that performing a set order of physical actions would summon up and bring to the surface emotional memories that were stored within the body. This was not just some random artistic principle that Stanislavsky was tinkering with. At this time the sciences, not just the arts, were undergoing a kind of revolution. Pavlov's pioneering work with dogs and the ability to condition their behaviors greatly impressed Stanislavsky. If dogs could be conditioned to have a pre-programmed response to a given stimuli, why not actors? Sonia Moore explains,

> Stanislavsky discovered that human behavior is a psycho-physical process, and scientists have since confirmed that paths of nerves unbreak-

ably connect by a thousand threads the physical and the psychological in a human being. For instance, if I raise a glass, which is a physical act, I do it for some inner psychological reason: I may be thirsty, or I may want to see what is in it. Every inner experience is expressed through a physical action.

Pavlov's teachings about conditioned reflexes became important during the same period as Stanislavky's own teachings did. Stanislavsky was searching for a conscious means to control the inner mechanism responsible for our emotional reactions. Pavlov and Secheno confirmed the correctness of Stanislavsky's thesis that the whole complex inner life of moods, desires, reactions, and feelings is expressed through a simple physical action. (Moore 1965)

Since the psychological and the physical in human beings is so inextricably intertwined, to truthfully perform a physical action on stage means that the actor's truthful and honest emotions cannot help but come along for the ride. The actor's unconscious emotions would be stirred each time, simply by performing a simple, easily replicated physical action. Performing this set physical actions would create the appearance of a genuine emotion without the actor needing to consciously delve deep within his psyche to retrieve a memory.

Stanislavsky cautioned that his method of physical actions was simply a tool, and not a recipe for the creation of theatre. It would only be successful if actors used it as a launching point for their own creativity. He felt that the method of physical actions was a bit like studying the grammar of a language. Simply knowing the grammar for a language does not mean that the speaker will express beautiful thoughts in that language; it only means that the speaker understands the language's rules. Similarly, his "grammar," the method of physical actions, could only be made into truthful and beautiful moments on stage by the actor's imagination (Sawoski).

THE PLAY'S THE THING . . .
Stanislavsky developed a way of breaking down and understanding a play

that forms the basis of our modern understanding of script analysis. He saw theatre as action (which is why we use the modern term **action-based acting** to describe his system and other systems influenced by his thinking). For Stanislavsky, the text was an identifiable series of actions and their consequences. Texts needed to be analyzed and understood inside-out by the actor. Early on in his career he favored lengthy table-work sessions with his actors where they dissected the script to uncover its action and meaning.

Six fundamental questions form the basis of Stanislavsky's approach to a text. We often refer to these in our modern acting classes as the **given circumstances**. They can be called by different names according to the style of different teachers, but their essence remains the same. The questions are:

- Who?
- Where?
- When?
- Why?
- For what reason?
- How?

Let's break these questions down even further:

Who

Who, specifically, is my character? What are the details of her life and background, and how does that shape her thinking and approach to the world?

Where

 In a large sense, this question can be "What country am I in?" while in a smaller sense we could ask, "Where am I within this room?" It is the actor's job to determine how the "where" of the scene affects the character and his behaviors.

When

When specifically is this action taking place? This question encompasses the "big when" (what year is it, what point in history is it?) as well as the "small when" (what time of day or night is it?). It is the actor's job to determine how the when affects her, from social mores of the time period to the atmosphere and ambience created by different times of the day or night. Time, in every sense, influences and affects behavior.

Why?

Why is this all happening now? What events have transpired that make what is going on now necessary? Why are you here? Unlike the "who," "where," and "when" answers, which are usually supplied by the play, this is a question that could have different answers depending on the actor's individual point of view.

For What Reason?

This question is also named by many current practitioners simply as "What?" This is a question that can't help but have a psychological basis, depending on the actor's choice. The question begs a clarification of what it is that you, the character, want. In many ways it seems remarkably similar to the "why" question, and yet it impels the actor to go even deeper psychologically. For what reason do you, the character, need this thing to be happening in the play? This is a slightly different question than "Why?" (which implies that the question to be answered is, "Why are these circumstances bringing you to this point of action?").

How?

With this question you are asking yourself, "How will you try to get what it is that you want"? The "how" is the most interesting of the questions, because, unlike the first three questions ("who," "where," and "when," usually answered by the playwright), and the next two questions ("why" and "for what reason," which can be decided upon by your imagination and set for the run of the play), the "how" question is ever changeable.

> "How" was clarified for me by another of my Russian mentors, acting master Albert Filozov. Filozov . . . believes that if you're truly alive to the myriad nuances of your fellow actors' behavior, then your "how" will never be fixed: it will inevitably and necessarily change each night or during each take at a minuscule level as you respond to *their* ever changing performances. (Merlin 2007)

BASIC PRINCIPLES OF UNDERSTANDING A TEXT

In addition to these six fundamental questions, Stanislavsky developed a way of breaking down and mapping out the text so that the actor could navigate its moment-to-moment journey through a progression of **beats** or **units**.

- A unit is a portion of a scene that contains one **objective** for an actor.
- An objective is the thing that the actor/character wants to get or accomplish. It is the character's goal—the thing that the character desperately needs. This objective or goal changes each time a shift occurs in the scene (**unit change** or **beat shift**).
- The character's objective is sought through an **action** (as expressed through the use of an active verb; for example, to berate, to empower, to placate). This action changes throughout the beat as the character tries various ways to obtain what he wants from another character on stage. The action (expressed as a verb) could be expressed and implemented physically.

An actor's journey through a play is more than a series of objectives unfolding sequentially. To help us see a play as a whole entity, rather than a series of strung-together events, Stanislavsky developed the idea of a **super-objective**—meaning the main thing that the character wants or needs over the entire course of the play. All individual beats, with their accompanying objectives and actions, when put together form the character's super-objective, that overarching desire or need. In addition to the objective of the individual scene (what the character wants and needs most in that moment), there is always the overarching objective (the thing that the character wants most over the course of the play).

The idea of the super-objective seems, very often, to stump actors. My colleague Terry Hardcastle described the idea of a super-objective very clearly:

> In the movie *Batman*, Batman's goal throughout the entire movie is to save Gotham. This is the big thing that he is working for. This is his super-objective. In an individual scene, his objective might be to get Catwoman on his side, or to kick Bane's ass, but these small scene-by-scene objectives are in service of his larger super-objective. He doesn't change his super-objective halfway through the movie and decide that his real goal is to get a Krispy Kreme doughnut.

STAGE TRUTH AND THE MAGIC OF THE MAGIC IF

Although Stanislavsky sought truth and a kind of realism on stage in his work, theatre, he acknowledged, was not a replication of real life but a heightened viewing of life. Theatre crystallized the most important and poignant moments of our humanity for the spectator to see. It was the actor's job to create an *appearance* of a truth on stage but not to *experience* that truth.

This notion is what lead Stanislavsky to create the **magic if**.

In the magic if, the actor puts himself in the position of the character: "*If* this same thing were happening to me, how would I react?" Putting oneself in the position of imagining "*If* I were this character, what would I do?" paved the way to a series of replicable physical choices by the actor that

would appear truthful and genuine to the audience without the actor need
ing to experience and live those emotions.

The beauty of the magic if is that it creates a safe wall of distance between the actor and the character. The actor does not pretend to be the character. An actor playing Medea does not believe herself to be Medea, but
rather poses the question to herself, "If I were to murder my children, what
would that be like and how would I react? What kinds of stuff might I physically do?" I am sure that you can see that the magic if is a sanity saver! If
the actor playing Medea had to actually make herself believe that she *was*
a child-murdering sorceress, you could see where that could create some
problems during her offstage time at home with her real-life family. They
would all be in need of some therapy. The magic if is a way of bridging the
gap between the actor's reality and the character's reality so that they never
became dangerously intertwined.

IMAGINATION AND SUBTEXT

Stanislavsky believed that the imagination was one of the actor's most powerful tools and as such must be constantly cultivated and challenged. Imagination is used to flesh out the details of the script and the character that the
playwright may have left unnamed or undeveloped. The playwright does
not necessarily provide a history or elaborate biography of each character.
It is up to the actor's imagination to fill in those gaps to create a fully developed human being with a past, a present, and possibly even an imagined
future. The actor must provide detail, using his imaginative powers, to create dimensional characters.

Stanislavsky believed that one of the most powerful tools for stimu-
lating and exercising the actor's imaginative powers was observation. The
actor needed to observe her surroundings carefully, and meticulously notice details of behavior and physicality in others. In addition, she needed to
spend an enormous amount of time simply watching and noting the world
around her in order to develop the vital tool of imagination. In Stanislavsky
training today, observation plays a vital role. Students are often asked to

observe people in real life in great detail, replicating their behaviors in detailed exercises.

However, Stanislavsky did not believe that imaginative powers should be used to attempt to *copy* reality. There was, to Stanislavsky's mind, a difference between actual reality and theatrical reality. We can think of stage reality as a kind of condensed and more intense version of reality. Stage reality selects the most heightened and poignant moments in life and presents them to the audience, omitting the minutiae or mundane moments of real life. For example, if an actor spends an hour observing a man on a park bench sleeping, he will keenly observe every detail of the man's behavior in life. On stage, however, the actor may only present the most interesting or notable aspects of his observation. The actor is not presenting or replicating the exact behavior that he observed in its entirety. Rather, he uses his imagination to select the most valuable and meaningful observations with which to create a believable, heightened stage reality, rather than to replicate life.

Another way in which the actor's imagination works to create nuanced characters is by filling in **subtext** in a play. Because characters, like human beings in real life, do not always speak their true thoughts aloud, an actor must imagine what her character is truly thinking and how she is trying to subtly affect other characters on stage. This is the character's subtext; that is, the meaning underneath the spoken words that contain the character's true nature and intentions. The playwright supplies the character's words, but not the thoughts underneath the words. It is the job of the actor to imagine those meanings, and to embed them in the vocal and physical life that she creates for the character.

Stanislavsky's growth as an artist and thinker was inextricably tied to the works of playwright Anton Chekhov, whose work was featured at the Moscow Art Theatre. Chekhov's plays used subtext extensively. What was being said by the characters on stage was the surface veneer, hiding their true meanings and passions. In Chekhov's plays even silences held a great deal of information about what the characters were truly experiencing and desiring. Chances are if a character in a Chekhov play is complaining about the weather, he is preoccupied with something other than rain or thunder. Polite social dialogue smoothed the surface of boiling passions and frustrations.

> Chekhov's characteristic method of creating a subtext is to suggest that his characters live two lives. One is the external life presented in the text which includes the characters' hopes, beliefs and aspirations, as well as their subjective view of themselves and of life. . . . Chekhov proceeded to create a perceptible gap between the subjective and objective lives of his characters. (Borny 2006)

The subtext, as Stanislavsky and Chekhov both saw, was the lifeblood of the play. As Stanislavsky once said, "Spectators come to the theatre to hear the subtext. They can read the text at home" (Moore 1984).

TEMPO-RHYTHM

In addition to knowing what vital things are unspoken by the character, to create a believable and truthful character the actor needed to develop an understanding of what Stanislavsky called **tempo-rhythm**. He believed that without understanding the character's tempo-rhythm, physical actions on stage could not be performed in a realistic and believable manner.

The terms "tempo" and "rhythm" come from the world of music. Tempo is the rate at which an action is performed (its speed), and rhythm is the pattern or intensity of that action. Tempo-rhythm then refers to the speed and patterns of a character's emotional, physical, and psychological movement. It is the delicate navigation between the actor's own internal sense of rhythm and pace and the character's rhythm and pace. Any New Yorker who has spent any time in the rural South on a hot day can attest to the fact that different people have different innate tempo-rhythms; that is, the relative rapidity or slowness of their mental state and the speed at which they perform any physical action. A New Yorker waiting for the subway who is late for work and just had a fight with his girlfriend is going to have a very different tempo-rhythm than an older Southern woman living in Alabama drinking lemonade on her porch and reading the paper on a sunny day. The rate at which characters experience and maneuver through life can be different, not only from one character to another character, but even within a single character throughout the journey of the play.

The actor's challenge is to find a way to negotiate between her own internal speed and tempo and that of the character. Stanislavsky believed that it was vital that the actor be able to understand her own internal rhythm before trying to explore the rhythm of a character:

> You must get accustomed to disentangling and searching out your own rhythm from the general, organized chaos of speed and slowness going on around you on the stage. . . . When actors have an innately right comprehension of what they are conveying to the public they instantly fall into a more or less rhythmic pattern of verbal and physical expression. This happens because the bond between rhythm and feeling is so very close. (Farrell 2010)

Stanislavsky believed that not only individuals but also emotions had their own rhythmic life and speed. Just as a piece of classical music has its own rhythmic journey and may move quickly or slowly, smoothly or choppily through a given section, so too an actor's actions may change their rhythmic expression over the course of a play. Tempo-rhythm then, is not only a negotiation between the actor's own internal sense of rhythm and speed and that of the character, but is also a quality that is variable and changeable as the character faces different wins and losses, triumphs, failures, frustrations, and joy along his path in the play.

PHYSICAL APPARATUS, RELAXATION, AND CONCENTRATION
In order to create a character, an actor has to develop a detailed and nuanced physical life on stage. The inner life of the character is vital to discover, but if that inner life cannot find outer expression, the audience will

never know anything other than the surface of the character. In order to fully present the physical embodiment of a character—the sum total of the actor's nuanced physical and vocal choices—an actor must develop her physical instrument.

Stanislavsky insisted that an actor's voice be trained just like a singer's voice. He often expressed frustration with the slowness and muddiness of his actors' speech and sough to train and develop their vocal instruments. In the same way, he knew that the physical instrument must be prepared to express whatever is called for in the realization of a character. In order to provide a neutral canvas on which to create a character who was physically, emotionally, and intellectually different from him- or herself, the actor needed to cultivate an expressive and flexible body and voice.

From his own experience on stage, Stanislavsky recognized that unnecessary physical tension was an enormous obstacle to creativity. Constrained by tension in the mind or body, an actor was not free to develop the physical life of a character. Therefore, Stanislavsky sought tools for a complete release of physical and mental tensions. The simple act of breathing, he saw, was a vital part of relaxation. Patterns of breathing affect mental and emotional states, and simply by altering breath patterns, an actor can alter the appearance and expression of emotion and thought.

Stanislavsky also held that actors could reduce tension by using tools for focusing and concentrating on stage. With this in mind, he developed the **circles of awareness** (also called **circles of attention** or **circles of concentration**—remember, all of these terms have been translated from the Russian, which accounts for their variability). The actor using this tool would focus on a small circle (himself and his immediate surroundings). Once he had focused entirely on his immediate circle, he would expand his awareness to take in a larger area. The actor could then shift his focus between the circle of self and immediate environment to the larger environment outside of himself. This ability to take his focus back and forth from the self to the greater world, Stanislavksy believed, would help the actor to achieve what he called **public solitude**.

Public solitude is, quite simply, the ability to behave in public, while being observed, as though one were in private and all alone. Stanislavsky recognized that an audience changed the actor's behavior. For example, the act of ironing a blouse changes its shape and nature enormously if our ironing board is placed on a stage in front of five hundred people. All of a sudden the solitary, meditative, and peaceful quality one might experience while ironing is made self-conscious by the addition of spectators. Circles of awareness allow an actor to remain conscious that she is on stage, while at the same being able to retreat to an inner sense of truthfulness, allowing her to believably create private moments in public.

COMMUNION AND ADAPTATION

Stanislavsky believed that in order to communicate with an audience an actor must communicate fully or have **communion** with his fellow actors. This meant listening at all times to the words and choices of one's fellow actors, and reacting truthfully to whatever their presence was communicating. Nuances in movement, gesture, or vocal life that change from one performance to the next would duly affect an actor's response. This kind of moment-to-moment relationship meant that scenes would be fluid rather than static, changeable rather than fixed, creating a more truthful theatrical reality. The actor had to **adapt** his performance in the moment, not only to truthfully react to what was being leveled at him by the other actors, but to keep hold of the objective of his scene and his super-objective in the play.

Studying the Stanislavsky System

So now you've been introduced to the basic principles of Stanislavsky, and to what some (though not its creator) call the Stanislavsky method. What's it like to train under this system, and where will you find it?

WHERE WILL YOU FIND THIS TRAINING?

The short answer is "everywhere." As I said at the outset, I am hard-pressed to find an idea in actor training, no matter how revolutionary or modern it may seem, that does not have its roots in Stanislavsky. The reason is simple: these ideas make sense. They are a workable and intuitive tool kit for any actor.

When I first started studying Stanislavsky technique, I was amazed to find that a name was being given and a process was being identified for things that I had been doing naturally as an actor for years. I think this resonance and truthfulness comes about because Stanislavsky was trying to find a way to articulate and name an intuitive process that he was already using as an actor, rather than to create a definitive system. The work provides ways of approaching the primary areas an actor must contend with on stage: action, physicality, and text, and relationship to self, environment, and one's fellow actors.

You are likely to find that many training programs and teachers will use Stanislavsky as a base, and meld it with other concepts or training methodologies. An eclectic approach to Stanislavsky is most common. A program may say that they are teaching Stanislavsky when they are, in fact, teaching his basic principles but putting their own stamp on it. This can be useful and wonderful, as Stanislavsky's ideas lent themselves to expansion by other thinkers and practitioners. I think, if I may be so bold, that Stanislavsky would have wanted it this way. His work was not static; it evolved, grew, and changed as he challenged his own ideas. I think he would be pleased that his "system" is not being taught for the most part as a gospel, but is serving as a base for other practitioners and thinkers to add to and adapt as they believe most effective.

There are many different ways to approach the teaching of Stanislavsky as there are programs and practitioners. The system is still being taught in Russia today under the master acting teacher/student model described in Stanislavsky's books. At the Moscow Art Theatre, birthplace of Stanislavsky's experimentation, you will find unadulterated Stanislavsky teaching—no other influences or systems creep in.

What's It Like to Train Under This System?

THE CRITICS

Since the Stanislavsky system forms the foundation, or at least serves as the inspiration or genesis, for nearly every training system in America, it is almost heretical to openly criticize it. The major reservation that you might encounter regarding Stanislavsky training is that it is somehow dated; that the ideas have not been modified for a long period of time and have not evolved past their initial stages. The major problem with Stanislavsky's work is that it is so widespread in modern American training systems, so ubiquitous, subject to so many different interpretations and extrapolations, that it may not *really* be Stanislavsky's "system" any longer.

THE FANS

The true beauty of Stanislavsky's work, when it is taught focusing on the later chapter of his career, is that it provides a way of working where the actor can "stay safe." What do I mean by this? Stanislavsky himself noticed that his earlier tools, specifically emotional memory, could be psychologically draining and damaging to the actor. The refinements that he made to his thinking by developing the method of physical action, in concert with many of his other tools, created a system whereby actors could stay psychologically healthy. Working under Stanislavsky's later principles, the actor needn't delve deep into some distant and troublesome past to create roles on stage. Instead, she can synthesize and replicate those emotions utilizing physical tools, allowing her to remain in the present and stay engaged, healthy and connected.

A training system or program that assists actors in developing a process where they can remain psychology healthy, not only for their period of craft training, but as they move through their careers, is a wonderful system indeed.

WHERE TO GO FOR MORE INFORMATION

So much has been written about Stanislavsky that it can be overwhelming.

Stanislavski: An Introduction, by Jean Benedetti, and *The Stanislavski System: The Professional Training of an Actor*, by Sonia Moore, are both fairly straightforward reads that will help you to understand his work.

If you are feeling patient (the translation is awkward sometimes), you may want to read Stanislavsky's ideas in his own (translated) voice. Of the three books that he wrote, *An Actor Prepares* is perhaps the best place to start, not only because it is the first in his series of books, but because I find it to be the most accessible of his writings. It is a good thing to read. It is always best to get your information right from the source.

But bring your M&M's . . .

4

Lee Strasberg
and the Method

It should be noted that in all the performing arts except acting, the artist has an instrument outside of himself which he learns to control. . . . The actor is both the artist and the instrument—in other words, the violinist and the violin. . . . The Method, therefore, is the procedure by which the actor can open control of his instrument, that is, the procedure by which the actor can use his affective memory to create a reality on stage. —LEE STRASBERG

Who Was Lee Strasberg?

Cofounder of the Group Theatre, artistic director of the Actors Studio, founder of the Lee Strasberg Theatre and Film Institute, and developer of the world-famous American school of acting known as the Method, Lee Strasberg is one of the most famous acting teachers of the twentieth century. From approximately 1950 until his death in 1982, there was no more influential teacher of acting. Strasberg's Method shaped an entire generation's perspective regarding acting on stage and film, stressing a sense of truth through the emotional reliving of memory. Every teacher and student of acting searches for this "sense of truth," of course, in their own way. But Strasberg more than any other teacher before or since stressed the pre-eminence of the actor's will. Through practice, Strasberg believed the actor could attune the desire to relive any important emotional experience from memory within the context of character and dramatic performance. Careful, judicious use of **affective (emotional) memory** would allow the actor to avoid clichés in performance and attain the self-confidence longed for by every artist.

Mere "imitation" of emotion for Strasberg was unacceptable; showing that you were upset by "pretending" to cry was sacrilege. Strasberg wanted his actors to relive memory in performance. His unique perception of Konstantin Stanislavsky's acting process challenged the standards of what had been considered "real" in acting and created a startling sense of naturalness heretofore never seen. Never before had anyone concentrated with such intensity (sometimes to the detriment of the playwright's words) on the importance of the actor's performance in bringing a drama to life. For Strasberg, without the revelation of inner truth by the actor, without her experience of authentic emotion, it mattered not how brilliantly a writer had written her play. The play would fall flat unless the beating heart of the actor sat at the head of the proverbial table. The axis on which a production spun was on the emotional integrity of the actor (Hardcastle 2013).

A Brief History of Strasberg and his Method

As we've already seen, by stressing imagination, relaxation, and concentration, Stanislavsky more than any other artist before or since systematized what the actor must do to create consistently authentic performances. Enter a young Lee Strasberg, born in Austria-Hungary, brought to the United States at the age of eight, and most curious about theatre (Hull 1985). Growing up in New York's Lower East Side, Strasberg saw Stanislavsky perform with his Moscow Art Theatre in 1923 and 1924. It changed his life. "I doubt that the minute, detailed, moment-to-moment aliveness on the stage represented by and participated in by every member of the cast will ever be achieved again," he wrote in his memoir (1988). When two of Stanislavsky's actors, Richard Boleslavsky and Maria Ouspenskaya, remained in America to start the American Laboratory Theatre in 1924, Strasberg signed up. By attending Boleslavsky's lectures and Ouspenskaya's acting classes, he was introduced formally to Stanislavsky's ideas (Blair 2010). The LAB, as it was called, became Strasberg's seminary (Hardcastle 2013). But it was Ouspens-kaya's in class work with actors that impacted him the most and would have the greatest influence on his later approach to actor training.

Called "Madame" by her students, Ouspenskaya had a piercing glare and a commanding presence (Frome 2001). Her vehement criticism could bring acting students to tears, but also broke down the student's inhibitions to make them more emotionally fluid. To the outside viewer, Madame might have looked like a meanie, but she wasn't; she just believed in "tough love." Madame conducted exercises involving concentration on objects for ten minutes at a time in order to memorize everything about the item (Strasberg 1988). This sharpened the actor's will to perform more difficult tasks, such as the use of affective memory. Affective memory, variously called emotional or emotion memory, was trained by creating high-stakes scenarios for the actor to perform. Stanislavsky's discoveries filtered through Ouspenskaya's unforgiving commitment to emotional realism were Strasberg's greatest inspiration. Soon thereafter, with friends Cheryl Crawford and Harold Clurman, he would use this inspiration to found two of the most important movements in American theatre: the Group Theatre and this other little something; maybe you've heard of it. It's really no big deal—just a little thing called the Method!

In 1931, Clurman, Crawford, and Strasberg joined with twenty-seven actors, including Stella Adler and Sanford Meisner, inspired by Clurman's vision of a theatre that served something larger than themselves (Hull 1985). By uniting under one umbrella of training (Strasberg's department) and sub-mitting themselves to the leadership of Clurman, Strasberg, and Crawford, this group of actors committed themselves to a true theatrical ensemble, something America, which celebrated the individual actor/artist, had never seen (Hardcastle 2013). Clurman was drawn to Strasberg's passion for "act-ing upon which," says Clurman, "he seemed as concentrated as a jeweler over the inner mechanism of a watch" (Clurman 1957). Strasberg, accord-ing to Clurman, believed the interpretive elements of a play (that is, the acting itself) contributed in a creative way to the overall production; that without this element most plays never rose to a high standard. To lean too heavily on the importance of the playwright's words, reducing plays to their literary traditions, could make a play boring (Clurman 1957). By stressing improvisation, Strasberg was encouraging a more intimate relationship to the play and gave his actors a greater stake in the quality of the outcome. Conducting rehearsals in this personal way led to the cornerstone of Strasberg's approach to acting forever more: his work with affective memory. For Clurman, Strasberg's work in this area was nothing short of miraculous.

> Here at last was a key to that elusive ingredient of the stage, true emotion. And Strasberg was a fanatic on the subject of true emotion. Everything was secondary to it. He sought it with the patience of an inquisitor, he was outraged by trick substitutes. . . . Here was something new to most of the actors, something basic, something almost holy. It was revelation in the theatre; and Strasberg was its prophet. (Clurman 1957)

After his time with the Group Theatre, Strasberg spent many years doing everything from directing screen tests for Twentieth Century-Fox to coaching actors on Broadway (Garfield 1980). In 1951, Strasberg was offered the post of artistic director at the two-year-old Actors Studio in New York City, a position that would make him the most famous acting teacher in the world (Garfield 1980). As longtime friend and legendary director Elia Kazan (1988) put it, once Strasberg was hired, "no one could have been more committed or devoted. Or valued by everyone there. . . . Respect became hero worship, and hero worship idolatry."

During the 1950s and 1960s, it was impossible to avoid the Studio's influence, and the Method was the zeitgeist. "Audiences—not theorists or partisans—have made the success of Actors Studio veterans from Karl Malden and Robert De Niro to Rod Steiger and Geraldine Page and so many others," said Strasberg (Hull 1985). Indeed, the list of American actors trained by Strasberg is impressive: Anne Bancroft, Roscoe Lee Brown, Ellen Burstyn, Jill Clayburgh, James Dean, Bruce Dern, Robert Duvall,

Sally Field, Jane Fonda, Ben Gazzara, Julie Harris, Dustin Hoffman, Celeste Holm, Kim Hunter, Lainie Kazan, Steve McQueen, Marilyn Monroe, Paul Newman, Al Pacino, Geraldine Page, Estelle Parsons, Jose Quintero, Kim Stanley, Maureen Stapleton, Rip Torn, Shelley Winters, and so many others. American theatre students no longer needed to feel inferior to their European cousins. Here was an American approach to acting that was vital, important, and sexy. Strasberg would later found the Lee Strasberg Theatre Institute (now known as the Lee Strasberg Theatre and Film Institute) with branches in New York and Los Angeles, allowing many more other actors to experience Strasberg's unique approach to Stanislavsky's teaching. Strasberg died in 1982. The story goes that when he sank to the ground, he was asked what was wrong. He said, "I'm experiencing a heart attack." Even at death's door, Strasberg was checking in with himself, exploring his senses to understand what it felt like to have an actual heart attack. Even in these last crucial moments, Strasberg was doing the necessary, important work of an actor. using his Method (Hardcastle 2013).

The Method

This is where things get dicey, my friends. You see, Stanislavsky's approach to acting was eventually referred to as his "system." Strasberg believed he was building on Stanislavsky's work and called his work "the Method." So, both men had "methods," and when an actor says he or she is "Method," you might have to ask which "method" he or she is using, Stanislavsky's or Strasberg's. In truth, both gentlemen are almost in complete alignment with one another, given the reverence Strasberg and his contemporaries gave Stanislavsky, with one noteworthy difference. Strasberg's Method is primarily focused on the means to achieve uninhibited, relaxed, concentrated performances leading to the reliving of memory, i.e., affective memory. Affective memory for Strasberg was the most compelling element of Stanislavsky's system, and he built his career exploring it. It is creating a performance out of the stuff of life. Affective memory is the bread and butter of Strasberg's Method.

Strasberg took years to develop his Method. Through experimentation and experience, Strasberg arrived at a progression of training for the actor to make her most capable handling the rigors of performance. The Method is difficult. It demands more from the performer than mere imitation or gesture. It requires a high degree of relaxation, concentration, and a willingness to relive personal memories, some of which may be unpleasant. Strasberg was adamant on this point. Imitating emotions was cheap and easy. Only by re-experiencing feelings could a sense of truth be brought to the stage. The Method demands of the actor regular practice, leading to an increased ability to be private in public. This level of self-involvement can be alternately exciting and boring by turns. But no one can begin to hope to re-experience emotion on stage if they are unwilling (or unable) to harness their talent in a focused and disciplined way. Therefore, the effort and time required to master this kind of work is a barrier to some.

So how does one practice Method acting? If you took an acting class in Strasberg's Method, what would it be like?

Classes taught in the Method generally last four hours. The first two hours are spent on relaxation and concentration. Strasberg believed stage fright, that is "tension," was the enemy of all artists. When we are tense, we lock in our emotions, we become inhibited, and our bodies don't respond efficiently to our will. Although tension is a natural response to the pressures of performance and impossible to dispel entirely, through a practiced, regimented approach to physical relaxation, the actor becomes mentally relaxed. "The actor becomes completely responsive," said Strasberg. "His instrument gives forth a new depth of resonance. Emotion that has habitually been held back suddenly gushes forth. The actor becomes real . . ." (Hull 1985).

Relaxation and concentration in a Method class traditionally begins with the actor sitting in steel folding chair. Strasberg reasoned that this was comfortable enough without being so comfortable to allow the student to fall asleep. With aid of the instructor, the student is asked to draw their attention to various places in the body where tension is said to reside. By moving the neck, shoulders, back, and hips in unconventional ways, one is attenuating one's own will toward the area of tension. Releasing this tension, can often bring an unexpected welling up of emotion. By expressing that emotion with a steady "aaaahhhhhh," the actor does three things simultaneously: she expresses the released emotion, freeing her inhibition, she controls the emotion by expressing it in a specific way (through the "aaahhhh") and she demonstrates for the teacher that she has control over her instrument. The instructor may test the student for how effectively she is relaxed by lifting an arm. If the arm remains in mid-air when released, the student is obviously not completely relaxed! By bringing full attention to her own body, by releasing physical tension and expressing pent-up emotion with the "aaaahhhh," the actor is exercising her will and preparing for concentration exercises.

Again, through many years of trial and error, Strasberg came up with a curriculum, a course of study, for the actor to work through when developing his concentration. Remember, the point of the Method is to relive experience and emotion. By developing concentration through the exercising of **sense memory**, the actor becomes emotionally fluid and "real." After having completed the relaxation exercise, the actor with the aid of the instructor will work on a specific sense memory exercise. It could be the recreation of a favorite breakfast drink or maybe an overall sensation like a warm shower or a cold rain. Just as a white-belt karate student needs to demonstrate proficiency with certain kicks and punches before receiving a yellow belt, Strasberg logically built his sequence of exercises leading from easily accessible, common place sensations to more exotic, complex ones. As the student demonstrates competency, he is moved on to the next exercise at the behest of the instructor. As the sequence continues, the link between affective memory and sense memory becomes quite plain. Completion of this sequence of sensory exercises, although possible to do in a reasonable amount of time, was not what was important to Strasberg. It was the regular, deliberate use of the will in accomplishing these exercises that made the actor a trained craftsman. Eventually, affective memory work is explored in an effort to find those memories that are strongest and most reliable. As the student brings in scenes he is working on for class or for professional work outside of class, the actor and instructor can work together to find the affective memories best suited for the student's work.

The second half of a Method class is devoted to scene work or monologue work. This work is anything of the actor's choosing, be it a role she wants to work on in her spare time or a role she has been hired to play in a film. The scene is presented for the instructor and other students. The actor communicates what specific challenges she is having with the scene and her desired outcome for taking on the scene. After a presentation, the teacher may ask to see the scene again, but will probably ask the actors to improvise the scene in an effort to discover something new between the two characters. Strasberg was a big believer in improvisation and used it regularly when directing plays or teaching classes. By unshackling oneself from the words of the playwright, the actor's instincts are permitted full expression. Character is felt rather than played, making the performance in large part intuitive and highly personalized. The character is drawn to self, making for a truthful performance. Every class is a complete work out of the actor's psychophysical being. For four hours, the actor tackles relaxation, concentration, and scene work with improvisation. By doing this twice a week, she comes to be ready for anything. She is trained to relax when needed, enabling the best performance always.

What's It Like to Train Under This System?
THE CRITICS

When the Group Theatre's first production, *The House of Connelly*, by Paul Green, opened on September 21, 1931, the show received twenty-two curtain calls (Hirsch 1984). Glowing reviews came from almost all New York's newspapers. Brooks Atkinson, legendary critic for the New York Times was effusive in his praise. "This new band of actors . . . have done an extraordinary thing. They have been arrogant enough to regard acting as an art," said Atkinson. Nonetheless, he goes on to say, "They are self-conscious at present. They play at a tempo that is almost dull, and in order to keep their performance honestly subdued they are frequently hard to hear in a large auditorium. . . . They may force the soul too much" (Hirsch 1984). As the popularity of the Method increased alongside the popularity of Actors Studio actors like Marlon Brando, James Dean, and Montgomery Clift, Atkinson's criticism would be echoed by other, more strident, critics. For some, Method acting would be seen as producing self-conscious, mumbling performances that betray the spirit of Stanislavsky's teaching. The Method, seen by some as self-indulgence void of fidelity to the text . . . or even to the work of one's fellow actors, gained itself many enemies.

Sometimes criticism of the Method was an honest expression of distaste; its psychoanalytic feel was unpalatable to some. But unfortunately, critiques of the Method often devolved into ad hominem attacks against the man who created it. Robert Brustein stands head and shoulders above most critics of Strasberg. Before launching drama programs at Harvard and Yale, Brustein was theatre critic for the *New Republic* and eviscerated most every play of the Actors Studio's inaugural (and final) season on Broadway (Brustein 1967). Brustein believed that the Method relies on the actor's own personality too much for characterization, ignoring of the individual and unique demands each play. Indeed, Brustein seemed to have a personal bone to pick with Strasberg, going so far as to dramatize the domestic life of Lee Strasberg and his family most unflatteringly in his play *Nobody Dies on Friday*. No one comes as close to hating Strasberg, the man and his Method, as Brustein. But some come close.

Dislike for the Method (or for Strasberg; sometimes it's hard to tell which one other's dislike most) can also be found from other acting teachers, Stella Adler being the most famous. She and Strasberg had a famous disagreement that resulted in a schism within the Group Theatre that changed the history of American acting training forever.

In 1934, Stella Adler and her then husband, Harold Clurman, made a pilgrimage to Russia to speak with Stanislavsky himself. Adler was being directed by Strasberg in a play called *Gentlewoman*, in which she played an emotionally reserved socialite (Frome 2001). Adler was an emotionally vital actor, theoretically a good fit for Strasberg's Method. But Strasberg felt her character should have none of the emotional fireworks Adler was naturally capable of performing. That's right: Strasberg was telling Adler to feel *less*. Adler agonized and argued fiercely with Strasberg over this point, finally coming to a place of self-doubt (Frome 2001). When Clurman and Adler met Stanislavsky in Paris, Adler confided that she felt his system was the source of her anguish (Garfield 1980). Stanislavsky worked with her for five weeks, conversing only in French (which Clurman understood). During these meetings, Stanislavsky emphasized action *over* emotion, a seemingly direct contradiction to the way Strasberg applied Stanislavsky's system. When Adler returned to America, she presented what she claimed were secretarial notes transcribing Stanislavsky's literal words on the subject (Garfield 1980). She announced that Strasberg, according to the Master, had been misusing affective memory, which in her eyes must have been a vindication for everything negative she felt about Strasberg's insistent use of it. Angered, Strasberg proclaimed Stanislavsky had gone back on himself (Garfield 1980).

This event in theatre history is as multilayered as it gets and draws the persistent interest of those individuals trying to make hay from how the Method is "right" or "wrong." When considering this piece of history, it's important to realize that only a very few people really know what happened. And as science now tells us, even memory is not particularly reliable when it comes to facts surrounding an event. So, I think it's important to remain humble when trying to piece together history from personal perspectives. Stella Adler, troubled by Strasberg's direction of her in *Gentlewoman*, sought out the high priest of Russian theatre to aid her performance. Strasberg, ordinarily an enabler of emotional volcanoes, has been trying to *tamp down* Adler's natural emotional abandon for the sake of the play *through* affective memory. Stanislavsky, for his part, felt confronted by a panic-stricken individual, begging him to save her from the results of his own system. "I wasted a whole month on it," said Stanislavsky. "It turned out everything she had learned was right" (Garfield 1980). That is to say, Stanislavsky thought Strasberg was right, but Adler somehow believed that Stanislavsky thought Strasberg was wrong. No game of "telephone" could have resulted in a greater degree of misunderstanding. But this does underscore the importance of personality in the development of each individual's school of thought. *Personality*—not art in this case, not ideology, but *personality*— can shape history.

It seems silly in a way to bog oneself down in how much this theatre teacher adhered to Stanislavsky's principles or how much that theatre teacher didn't. Meisner, Adler, Strasberg, Chekhov, and all the great acting teachers inspired by Stanislavsky have more in common than not. Slavish adherence to another artist's principles is a dubious virtue. No painter ever proclaimed, "If you don't paint like Picasso, you're not a real painter." Strasberg from about 1934 onward forged his own path, creating his Method, a process so inspiring it influenced an entire generation of theatre artists and created some of the greatest film performances of the twentieth century. Criticisms regarding his adherence or lack thereof to Stanislavsky's system, in this light, seem parochial, as do the personal attacks against the man. Each teacher, each actor, each artist must at the end of the day pursue his own passion. Inspired by those who came before, but led by the heart, the artist holds a lantern out before him, walking, searching the path for one's own truth.

THE FANS

The saying goes that the proof is in the pudding. If there is anything valuable that an actor can learn from studying Strasberg's Method, it must come through in her performance. Academics can argue about which teacher is most true to Stanislavsky's System, whose teaching is "better" more "right," but the performance an actor gives in front of a live audience, or, in the case of a film, in front of cast and crew in often challenging settings or environments, is where the rubber meets the road. Take a look at James Dean in any one of the three films he shot in his short life, *East of Eden*, *Rebel Without a Cause*, and *Giant*. Is there ever a moment when you can catch him acting? How about Robert De Niro in *Taxi Driver*? Is there any artifice to Dustin Hoffman in *The Graduate* or *Kramer vs. Kramer*? Is there anything false about Paul Newman in *The Verdict*? When you watch Al Pacino in either one of the *Godfather* films, is there ever a moment when you see him slip? Especially when he shares scenes with his acting teacher, Lee Strasberg, in *The Godfather Part II*, is there a scintilla of artifice in either performance? If you are a fan of any of these actors, whether you recognize it or not, you're a fan of the Method.

Al Pacino lobbied for Lee Strasberg to perform the role of Hyman Roth in *The Godfather Part II*. Strasberg could have declined to risk his reputation on the role. Instead, he decided to expose himself, the artistic director of the Actors' Studio, high priest of the Method, to all the critics that would surely line up to see if he could practice what he preached. Even his most unforgiving critics had to sheath their stilettos. Strasberg ably demonstrated the technique he had created, earning himself an Academy Award nomination for Best Actor in a Supporting Role along with his former students Robert De Niro and Michael V. Gazzo. When De Niro won the award, the teacher was generous. "I knew Bobby should win," he said (Adams 1980). Also noteworthy is Strasberg's performance in *Going in Style*. Performing alongside two of the most un-Method performers one can imagine (a brilliant George Burns and Art Carney), Strasberg demonstrates the Method need not be all storm and stress. Strasberg's comedic performance is as funny as it is heartfelt: the Method in Groucho glasses.

It is not an accident that so many successful film actors came from the Actors Studio. Stressing relaxation and concentration, leading to a sense of natural expression, the Method works very well on film. Film rewards a lack of actor energy, punishes tension, and exaggerates every falsehood. The Method, by encouraging the performer to practice sense and affective memory, leads to an increased ability to be private in public. By awakening one's will and training it to focus on the important stuff through sense memory work, by decreasing the detrimental effect of distractions during performance, the Method holds many rewards for the practitioner, not the least of which is an increased sense of self-confidence. By diminishing the deleterious effect of stage fright, by sharpening the will through regular relaxation and concentration exercises, by accessing affective memory through sense memory, a student of the Method may find not only a rewarding career as an actor, but a rewarding life in general. Learning about one's own inner mechanism, the thoughts and memories that hold the most importance, can only lead to being a more integrated, honest human being. Perhaps self-exploration is the scariest thing of all. But, for the fearless heart, the true actor who is willing to unlock these most personal of memories, there is treasure, the gold every actor longs for: the True Moment.

WHERE TO GO FOR MORE INFORMATION

So you want to know more about Method . . . take some Method acting classes! Acting is doing. If you are to have an informed opinion about Method acting, you must actually do it. If someone offers you an opinion about the Method, ask them where and with whom they studied. If you are a curious, intelligent, and talented actor (and you are!), I highly suggest you take some classes in the Method so you can find out firsthand the rewards of practicing it. Like scuba-diving, bull fighting, or playing paintball, reading or listening isn't the same as doing.

Strasberg died before his autobiography could be finished. A friend of the family, Evangeline Morphos, edited his notes into a comprehensive account of Strasberg's journey. In his own voice, Strasberg speaks to his earliest influences, his cofounding of the Group, and of course, his legendary work at the Actors Studio with the Method. Occasionally dry in delivery and style, but enormously informative and sure to be of interest to the student of theatre history, the book is *Lee Strasberg: A Dream of Passion*.

Lorrie Hull, onetime teacher at the Lee Strasberg Theatre and Film Institute and UCLA, as well as a student of Strasberg's, compiled his curriculum into a highly organized and detailed volume. If you can't take a Method acting class, reading her book is the next best thing: *Strasberg's Method as Taught by Lorrie Hull*.

Compiling transcripts from a series of videotaped lectures presented at his institute shortly before he died, Lola Cohen reveals a true man of the theatre. Strasberg's knowledge and firsthand account of his contemporaries and appreciation for them reveals a gentler, more generous Strasberg than his reputation allows. Take a look at Cohen's *The Lee Strasberg Notes*.

There's no better way to learn the Method than to take classes from those who studied with him. Try the Lee Strasberg Theatre and Film Institute in New York or West Hollywood. You can find out more at www.strasberg.com. The Institute also offers classes in movement, voice, acting for the camera, and stage combat.

Lorrie Hull and Dianne Hull teach Method classes all over the world. Both were students of Strasberg and follow his curriculum to the letter. You can find out more at www.methodactingclassesla.com or on their Twitter account, lorriehull@lorriehull.

5

Practical Aesthetics Technique

Always tell the truth. It's the easiest thing to remember. —David Mamet

The Practicality of Practical Aesthetics

A Practical Handbook for the Actor, which is the handbook, guide, and first and final word on the Practical Aesthetics approach to acting, opens with this quotation. It is taken from the play *Glengarry Glen Ross,* by David Mamet. From the choice of this quotation, and the word "practical" in the title of the technique itself, it is easy to get the gist: this is a no-nonsense, simple, pragmatic approach to acting technique.

The handbook has a committee of authors: Melissa Bruder, Lee Michael Cohn, Madeleine Olnek, Nathaniel Pollack, Robert Previto, and Scott Zigler. The book was written by this group of young actors almost as an antidote to other acting techniques, or at least as a correction to the often misguided or unclear teachers of these techniques. The authors felt that such training failed to provide actors with a dependable and useful set of tools. Their goal was to develop a concise, direct, and clear method of working that could be easily accessed by any actor.

Although it was a group of young, up-and-coming actors who distilled these ideas into a book, this acting technique was originally conceived of by David Mamet (the playwright whose quote appears above) and the actor William H. Macy, who with Mamet founded the Atlantic Theatre

Company. An essayist, director, and screenwriter, Mamet has worked on films including *The Untouchables, Hannibal,* and *Ronin.* As for William H. Macy, even if you don't think that you know who he is, I bet that you'd recognize his face from many movies. You are most likely to have seen him as Jerry Lundegaard in *Fargo* and "that guy" in *Boogie Nights, Magnolia,* and *Pleasantville,* just to name a few.

It is no surprise that a technique that aspires to be simple, clear, and concise started with no-frills kinds of people. David Mamet's signature— his style of writing—is quick and terse, conversational and clipped. He has often criticized other writers for writing dialogue that does not ring true as speech you might actually hear in life. Mamet's characters interrupt one another; dialogue overlaps; sentences and thoughts are unfinished or trail off. His style has become so distinctive that it is often referred to as "Mamet speak." Here is a good example of Mamet's style of dialogue, from a short play called *4 a.m.* (Mamet 1994).

> INT. Uh-huh . . . *(Pause.)*
>
> CALLER Greg?
>
> INT. Yes? *(Pause.)* I'm listening.
>
> CALLER Greg . . .
>
> INT. Yes?
>
> CALLER In the wr . . .
>
> INT. Yeah. I got it. Go on.
>
> CALLER In the . . .
>
> INT. No, no. No. Go *on.* I *got* it. Arnold Toynbee, human life on . . .
>
> CALLER As we're made of molecules, Greg, and the *atoms* of all human life that ever lived are still in all of us . . .
>
> INT. Okay, I got it. They exist, they've just been rearranged. *(Pause.)*
>
> CALLER Yes. *(Pause.)*

As you can see, Mamet is interested in replicating authentic human experience; he seeks to create truthful conversations among believable characters. For Mamet, the story is all, and flowery, poetic dialogue gets in the way of storytelling. Practical Aesthetics Technique and the Atlantic Theatre Company hold the story of the play to be the central creative force in a work of theatre. The main artistic voice belongs to the playwright, not to the director or the actor, whose primary creative purpose in this way of working is to serve the writer.

Where Did It All Begin?

It may sound as if Practical Aesthetics originated solely with Mamet, Macy, and the assorted actor-authors that I've mentioned, but its roots actually go far deeper. Practical Aesthetics is based on the teachings of quite the combination of players: Stanislavsky, Sanford Meisner, and the stoic philosopher Epictetus. You would never find these three together at a party. We already talked about Stanislavsky in this book, and later on we're going to talk about Meisner, but since Epictetus was a first-century Greek philosopher and not a theatre guy and, unlike William H. Macy, you probably never saw him or heard of him, he deserves a mention here.

The Enchiridion (a fancy Greek word for "handbook") is a summary of Epictetus' teachings. Epictetus was a Stoic philosopher, and this brief work is considered to be the core work of Stoic philosophy. The Stoics were a group of thinkers who were interested in determining the principles of proper conduct and the impact of "right" ethical and moral thinking on human freedom. The Stoics believed that destructive emotions were born of poor judgment, and that a wise person living an ethically and morally correct life would not suffer such emotions. Reasoning, they thought, could free one from destructive emotional behavior and help one to lead a more productive, peaceful, and harmonious life.

Old Epictetus begins *The Enchiridion* with this statement (Carter 2011):

> Some things are in our control and others not. Things in our control are opinion, pursuit, desire, aversion, and, in a word, whatever are our own actions. Things not in our control are body, property, reputation, com-

mand, and, in one word, whatever are not our own actions. The things in our control are by nature free, unrestrained, unhindered; but those not in our control are weak, slavish, restrained, belonging to others.

Wise words, Epictetus, wise words. But what does this have to do with acting?

It actually has everything to do with acting! On my first day of acting class at the American Repertory Theatre, when Scott Zigler (one of my former teachers and one of the authors of *A Practical Handbook for the Actor*) gave us Epictetus' writing, I don't think that I fully made the connection between the words of a Greek Stoic and the life of a modern actor. It was only years later that I put the pieces together. Really, an old Greek guy living and writing in the first century in Greece had a lot of good, sound advice for actors. The core of this philosophy informs Practical Aesthetics in every way. The voice of our friend Epictetus comes through in all of Practical Aesthetics' ideas.

ACTION AND PREPARATION

Epictetus says that all we can control is our thoughts and our actions. We cannot control our emotions or others' perceptions of us. In short, we cannot manipulate anything outside of ourselves, and believing that we can produces disharmony within us. Focusing on what we cannot control entraps us and limits our freedom, while focusing on our own judgment and actions (things within our control) frees us to act.

An actor embraces this freedom on stage through taking action rather than dwelling on an emotional experience. Because he can control only his own craft and preparation, the actor approaches artistic freedom by focusing his effort on strengthening his craft and instrument rather than worrying about outcomes over which he has no control (Carter 2011).

While Practical Aesthetics, as a "playwright-centered" philosophy, limits itself to working with the *text* of a play, it acknowledges the importance of voice and movement training. It does not offer the actor a system for doing this kind of preparatory work, as a more "actor-centered" approach might do; yet it holds this preparation to be part of the "proper and right" conduct that allows an actor to be at one with the play and the playwright's vision. Just as Epictetus believed that living a life of moral and ethical correctness equips a person to enter the world freely and to deal peacefully and productively with all that may arise, so too an actor who prepares her body and mind to go on stage is free to tackle all of the circumstances that may present themselves.

THE NUTS AND BOLTS

Now that we have looked at the philosophies that drive Practical Aesthetics Technique, we can look into the technique itself. The technique really falls into two main categories: analysis of the text and techniques for performance.

UNDERSTAND WHAT MAKES A GOOD PHYSICAL ACTION ON STAGE

A Practical Handbook for the Actor defines acting this way: "Acting is living truthfully under the imaginary circumstances of the play" (Bruder et al. 1986). This is an idea developed by Stanislavsky that is echoed here.

In order to live truthfully under the imaginary circumstances of the play, the actor needs to find the underlying physical action of the scene. An action is an idea, coming from Stanislavsky's technique, of what one character on stage does to another character in order to achieve his objective; that is, his goal or what he wants to achieve in the scene. Quite simply, Practical Aesthetics defines an action as "the physical pursuance of a specific goal" (Bruder et al. 1986). In *A Practical Handbook for the Actor*, nine criteria are given to help actors to find a good and playable action.

The action

1. Must be specific
2. Must be physically capable of being done

3. Must be in line with the playwright's intentions
4. Must not be emotionally or physically manipulative
5. Must not predetermine an emotional state
6. Must have its test in the other person
7. Must be fun to do
8. Must not be an errand
9. Must have a "cap" (a way of finishing)

These nine criteria are the benchmark, this technique says, of finding a good playable action on stage. Again, the word that we use here is "action." Action is something that the actor can think through and do, on stage, unlike playing an emotional state, which is a state of being that is outside of the actor's realm of control.

ANALYZING THE SCENE

Developing an understanding of what makes a good action is only one part of the equation, however. An actor has to learn which action is best used for a given scene. In order to do that, she has to closely analyze the play and each scene.

Practical Aesthetics has the actor break down a script according to three questions. The actor must read the script carefully and ask herself:

1. What is the character literally doing?
2. What is the essential action of what the character is doing in the scene? That is, what does the character really want the other character to say or do?
3. What is the action like to me? It's as if . . . (Do you remember Stanislavsky's magic if? It's kind of like that. The essential action needs to relate to the actor's own life so that the actor can access a personal truth in the scene).

Let's look at these ideas in a little bit more depth.

Question #1

This is not a tricky or clever question. It is intended to elicit a statement of what the character is literally—not metaphorically—doing throughout the scene. It may be something as simple as "two sisters are discussing how to handle their mother's illness." By literally describing what is going on in the scene, the actor boils the scene down into its clearest, most basic terms so that she can always keep in mind the story that is being told to the audience.

Question #2

This is a way of distilling the essence of what is being sought in the scene. It is a way of describing, not the literal action of what is happening, but the interpersonal juice that drives the scene forward. For example, if the literal description of the story above is "two sisters are discussing how to handle their mother's illness," then the essential action of that scene might be "to beg a loved one to step up to the plate."

Question #3

This last question engages the actor's imagination. It is a way of asking oneself, "If I were in this position (the position that the character is in) and undertaking this action (the action that I am pursuing in the play), what would this be like for me?" This allows the actor to link personal experience to the play and to "live truthfully under imaginary circumstances." Without linking the imaginary circumstances to personal experience, it would be difficult to make the actions believable and honest.

By focusing on these three steps, we can see that Practical Aesthetics is an entirely action-based process. Any emotion that seems to arise in the actor on stage is what I'll call a "by-product"; that is, an emotional state on stage is not what is being sought after or pursued by the actor. Rather, one may see an emotion arise in an actor or actors on stage while a goal is diligently being pursued.

Techniques for Performance

If the actor's job is to "live truthfully under the imaginary circumstances of the play," the success or failure of that truth is entirely dependent on what is going on moment to moment in the play as it unfolds on stage on any given afternoon or evening. For the actor to respond truthfully in the moment, he must listen. The actor places his focus, not on himself, but on the other actor. As Scottish director Mark Westbrook explains,

> The actor employing Practical Aesthetics is in a constant state of improvisation. Each moment on stage is unrehearsed in the traditional sense. Instead, rehearsal writes into the muscle memory of the actor the given circumstances of the play, including notes from the director and tools or tactics by which to pursue an essential action for each scene. In Mamet's words "we prepare to improvise." Lines are learned by rote without meaning or feeling. This allows the individual line to serve any possible tactic without fixing a line reading.

In order to do this, the actor must place his entire focus and attention on the other actor. This means that the actor must receive the scene partner's energy and be changed by it. While an actor can prepare by understanding the play and asking the series of questions that we discussed above, he or she must remain flexible and able to adapt to the truth of the moment as it changes and develops. If the actor is truly engaged in listening to the scene partner or partners on stage, the possibilities for the scene and the play are endless. The performance will never be the same twice.

STUDYING PRACTICAL AESTHETICS

So now you've been introduced to the basic principles of Practical Aesthetics. I like to think that it is really an attempt to distill the Stanislavsky system with a few of its own twists.

What's It Like to Train Under This System?

THE CRITICS

Critics of Practical Aesthetics Technique seem to have two chief misgivings.

1. The technique is overly "cerebral"; that is, it is logical a
    nd measured, and that this degree of intellectual control
    rules out passion on stage.
2. The technique is somehow "anti-actor."

Let's take a quick look at the last statement. These are words taken from the introduction to *A Practical Handbook for the Actor*:

> Talent, if it exists at all, is completely out of your control. Whatever talent might be, you either have it or you don't, so why waste energy worrying about it? The only talent you need to act is a talent for work-ing—in other words, the ability to apply yourself in learning the skills that make up the craft of acting. To put it simply, anyone can act if he has the will to do so, and anyone who says he wants to but doesn't have the knack for it suffers from a lack of will, not a lack of talent. (Bruder et al. 1986)

It is true that talent is outside of one's control, and it is true that hard work and preparation are all that are within our control. Worrying about one's degree of talent is, no doubt, a waste of energy since it is a factor that no degree of worrying, thought, exploration, or conclusions can change.

While one cannot argue with the truthful nature of the idea that talent is outside of one's control and it is a misdirection of mental resources to bother thinking about it, and no one can argue with the notion that hard work and applying oneself to learning the craft of acting are vital to being a good actor, there have been many who bristle at the rest of these ideas. The proponents of Practical Aesthetics state that if talent doesn't really exist or matter, then *anyone* can be an actor with proper training and discipline. There are many who feel that this notion undermines the value and artistry of the actor; that Practical Aesthetics treats the actor, not as an artist with a voice in her own right, but as a tool to serve the voice of the true artist, the playwright. Mamet has been roundly criticized and labeled "anti-actor" for his emphasis on story and playwright and his de-emphasis of the voice and creative contribution of the actor. One could make the case that he is not he is not "anti" anything but rather that he is "pro-playwright" and "pro-storytelling." As coach Mark Westbrook explains,

> To the Practical Aesthetics actor, there is no character. It cannot be created; the writer has already given you everything you need to act the role by suggestions made in the script. The illusion of character is created when the writer's words mix with the performer's actions and is born in the audience's mind. The Practical Aesthetics trained actor does not look for emotional connection to the text or character; instead, they find the commonality in action. We are interested in how the character fulfills their intent. It is about truthfully carrying out the character's actions, although note that we are not talking about walking, talking, or eating breakfast; we are talking about objectives fueled by intention and manifested through the truthful performance of psychophysical actions. (Westbrook 2010)

THE FANS

Although I'm sure die-hard Practical Aesthetics folks would hunt me down and skin me alive for putting it this way, I personally like to think of Practical Aesthetics as "Stanislavsky Lite." The basic principles here are much the same as those of our Russian friend Konstantin, only the system is boiled down to core principles and techniques, all of them script- and story-centered. The technique is simple. Fans like its straight-forwardness; it is pragmatic and (pardon my French) "bullshit free." Like all systems, it demands that the actor be disciplined, that she divest herself of bad performance habits that make it hard to be present on stage in the moment.

Compared to Stanislavsky's system, Practical Aesthetics is quicker to get under one's belt. Its tools are practical and immediate; one can take its ideas and immediately apply them to a specific job at hand. The system reflects the no-nonsense, no-mystery, roll-up-your-sleeves-and-get-down-to-work nature of its creators.

It may not be the best training tool for every actor, but for a certain kind of straightforward, practical actor, it just might be the tool kit that makes the most sense.

WHERE TO GO FOR MORE INFORMATION

The best thing to do to really get a firm command of this system is to read the book *A Practical Handbook for the Actor.* You may also wish to read the books of Robert Cohen, one of the handbook's many authors, beginning with *Acting Power.* David Mamet's book *True and False: Heresy and Common Sense for the Actor* may also be of interest. And if you like a no-nonsense approach, Mark Westbrook's online book, *Truth in Action,* is about as no-nonsense as they come.

Training courses in Practical Aesthetics Technique seem to be popping up in more places these days, not all of them in America. I often see online information for classes in Australia and Scotland. You may want to look into PAA (Practical Aesthetics Australia) and ACS (Acting Coach Scotland).

In the US, perhaps the best place to go for training in this technique is the Atlantic Acting School, which is associated with the Atlantic Theatre Company and is the training ground for this technique. It is always a great idea to study a technique as close to its original source as possible. The school offers a variety of programs outside of its theatre conservatory, including summer intensives and evening programs, with training sites in New York, Vermont, Los Angeles, and Australia. You can read about them at www.atlanticactingschool.org/about.

The American Repertory Theatre Institute for Advanced Theatre Training at Harvard University also offers training in this technique (as well as other techniques derived from Stanislavsky).

Michael Chekhov
Technique

The imagination of an actor is not that of an ordinary person. I want to know how to do things which I am not able to do. The moment I begin to concentrate on an object I begin to use my imagination, and it becomes something else.

—Michael Chekhov

In life, it's not always what you know but whom you know. The world of theatre is all about connections. This is not a modern development. Let's look at the great acting teacher and theorist Michael Chekhov. If his last name sounds familiar to you, there's a good reason for that. His uncle was the great Russian playwright Anton Chekhov. Like all young actors, Michael Chekhov had talent and needed a break. When he had been studying on his own for four years, passionate about acting and devoted to it, Anton Chekhov's widow, Olga Knipper, made an important introduction. Twenty-year-old nephew Michael was introduced to Konstantin Stanislavsky. The world of theatre changed because of that meeting.

Michael Chekhov was Stanislavsky's most talented student. A strange thing sometimes happens between mentors and their protégés. The very thing that attracts the mentor to the protégé—namely the student's intellect, talent, and strength—can ultimately turn the student, once educated, into something of a rival. Once the protégé's talent is developed and he comes into his own as an artist and intellectual, the master teacher can be questioned and challenged.

Such was the case with Chekhov and Stanislavsky. Trained by Stanislavsky, Chekhov rose from total obscurity as an actor and creative artist to something of a rival in a very short period of time. Eventually, Chekhov began to question and reject some of Stanislavsky's core principles.

If you remember our chapter on Stanislavsky, you'll recall that he loathed the untruthful stage behavior of his time and turned to realism and naturalism in his work. While Michael Chekhov, as a student of Stanislavsky, also valued truth on stage, he began to find the constraints of realism limiting. Stanislavsky, you may recall, embraced science and its teachings on psychology (remember his fascination with the work of Pavlov, who trained dogs to salivate) to help actors to understand character. Michael Chekhov believed more in the power of imagination and inspiration to create character. For Chekhov, the theatre needed to be more than a replication of life; it needed to be something greater and more inspiring. Life on stage needed to be a heightened reality, rather than reality itself. While this was a goal Chekhov shared with Stanislavsky, he and his former mentor had different ideas about how to achieve it. Stanislavsky emphasized the power of research and analysis. To understand the role and to bring truth to it, the actor had to gain an in-depth understanding of the script, dig deep into the inner workings of the character, and understand the given circumstances. Chekhov, on the other hand, believed that the best place to start to create a truthful performance on stage was not with research, but with imaginative power.

Basic Principles

Chekhov developed acting techniques that integrated the actor's body and psychology in a way that had not been done before. He termed his technique a **psycho-physical** approach, one that connected impulse and imagination. Its core principle is that the body affects psychology, and psychology affects the body.

The following elements form the core of Chekhov's teachings. They are all explained in depth in his books *On the Technique of Acting* and *Lessons for the Professional Actor*. Different teachers of Chekhov technique will chose to focus on different elements. Some may even use slightly different terminology to give form to his teachings. The following are some, but not all, of his basic principles as set forth in his book *To the Actor* (later compiled and translated into *On the Technique of Acting* [1991]).

PSYCHOLOGICAL GESTURE

Chekhov believed that the body and the mind were inseparably linked and interdependent. The physical body influenced psychology and psychology influenced the physical body in an unending feedback loop. **Psychological gesture** is a term coined by Michael Chekhov and a foundational concept in his technique. The psychological gesture is an outer movement that expresses inner psychology of the character. The National Michael Chekhov Association explains it like this:

> Chekhov defines the psychology to consist of the thoughts, feelings, and will of a human being. Hence, the psychological gesture is a physical expression of the thoughts, feelings, and desires of the character, incorporated into one movement. You can liken it to a moving logo, like the Nike logo, which captures the essence of Nike in one image. So, in one movement, the psychological gesture awakens the essence of the character in you thus aligning your thoughts, feelings and will (objective) with that of the character. When this happens, your walk, your expressive mannerisms, your voice and line delivery are all inspired by one moving image.

It works like this: The actor performs this gesture prior to the beginning of the scene to help her to find the essential nature of the character. During the course of the scene, if the actor falters, becomes distracted, or just feels "off," she may return to this gesture to connect herself with the character.

For example, if an actor is playing a character who has recently gained a great deal of weight but wishes to feel sexy, the psychological gesture she may develop is a repeated smoothing of the sides of her skirt. With this one gesture the actor can encapsulate a world of psychology and behavior. The gesture communicates a concern about her body image, a desire to feel appealing, and a need to be attractive to others. In short, this one gesture sums up the objectives and psychology of the character quickly, putting the actor in touch with key details in an instant.

IMAGINATION AND IMAGINARY BODY

Chekhov believed that all acting was completely dependent, not on the actor's intellect, but on his capacity for imagination. The greater the actor's imaginative powers, the more compelling the role. Chekhov believed that the imagination was not only an innate gift but also a tool that could be strengthened and trained.

Often the actor is called upon to play a character that is very physically different from himself. Chekhov believed that the actor could learn how to inhabit a different person's body and features by clearly visualizing it and stepping into that imagined body.

To do this, the actor imagines, in great detail, this other physical body. It can be created in front of him as he imagines sculpting a statue from a lump of clay or chiseling a block of marble to create this new person. Once the character is fully envisioned, the actor moves his real, tangible physical body into this imagined body. The imagined body may be shaped quite differently from the actor's real body. The center of gravity and means of motion for the imagined body might be drastically different from the actor's own. For example, the actor in real life might be thin and have a high center of gravity, pitching the body slightly forward and leading himself through space from his shoulders, while the imagined body might be heavier and stockier, the center of gravity lower. This character might move through space initiating movement from his hips and thighs. Whatever the distinction between the imaginary body and the actor's real body, this tool enables the actor to find, not only a physical difference between himself and the character, but the ways in which such physical differences manifest themselves psychologically.

COMPOSITION

It is interesting to me that Chekhov wrote about **composition**. To me, it seems a very forward-thinking element, one that looks beyond the work of an actor and examines how the actor fits into a bigger picture. Composition examines how artistic elements are arranged. The arrangement of objects and bodies in space on stage guides both the actor and the spectator, structuring their experience. For Chekhov, composition made life on stage dimensional and true.

ATMOSPHERE

Chekhov looks at **atmosphere** in two senses: atmosphere of place, which the actors and the audience see or hear, and psychological atmosphere, which they feel. The atmosphere of place affects the psychological atmosphere. The converse is true as well; the atmosphere of the characters' psychology influences the feeling of the place.

For example, I was in a production of the play *Macbeth*. In it, we cornered the market on dry ice and fog machines. Our production created a physical atmosphere: an otherworldly, dark and mysterious place where fair was foul and foul was fair. That physical atmosphere created a psychological atmosphere of darkness and evil. This can work equally powerfully in reverse, where a character's psychological atmosphere shapes and changes the place. In Shakespeare's *King Lear*, the emotional storm inside King Lear's head (after he has lost his kingdom, his dignity, and his sanity) manifests itself as a literal storm upon a heath.

QUALITIES (SENSATIONS AND FEELINGS)

"Feelings cannot be commanded, they can only be coaxed," Chekhov wrote in *On the Technique of Acting* (1991). In contrast, "Qualities are immediately accessible to you—especially to your movements." What does this mean? As an actor, I may not feel anger, but by repeatedly moving my body with a quality of anger (for example, pounding my fist into a pillow repeatedly), eventually a feeling of anger may be summoned. Similarly, if I reach out my hand to someone on stage with a gesture of love, happiness, or forgiveness, the quality of my movement may ultimately generate the feeling associated with it.

FEELING OF EASE

As an actor, being told to "relax" always made me do quite the opposite; I would immediately go stiff in my body. It's a lot like saying, "Try not to think about pink elephants." What do you immediately think about when you hear this? Pink elephants. Chekhov knew that the actor must find a **feeling of ease** from within, rather than having the idea of being relaxed imposed from the outside. Working with ease is not only critical for the actor to be able to do his best work, but necessary for the audience. I remember watching a play in Romania in which an actor walked across a narrow railing carrying a lit candle and a great deal of tension. As a result, the audience (at least this pyro-petrified, safety-conscious American) was taken out of the action of the play. In the absence of a sense of ease, the person on stage was no longer the character, but an actor whose safety was in question. Chekhov knew that when the actor worked from a sense of ease, the spectator could more easily buy into the truth of the stage action.

FEELING OF STYLE

Chekhov knew the limitations of realism and naturalism. He recognized that there were other styles of theatre. By encouraging his actors to work with a **feeling of style**, Chekhov acknowledged that there is no one, singular reality for all plays. He saw that plays could have different kinds of realities, and that different realities of different styles of theatre had their own rules and modes of being. For example, we know that if we go to see an action movie, the world that we will enter as spectators will be drastically different than if we go to see a romantic comedy, a documentary, or a drama. Different genres of movies have different rules of reality. In an action movie, we know that after a car chase people can walk away from the crashed car unscathed, making witty remarks; in a drama they cannot. Chekhov recognized that not all theatrical experience needed to adhere to one particular style or set of theatrical rules for the world that was created on stage. It was the actors' job to feel and understand the world that they were entering into.

FEELING OF FORM

Form is how we understand things. It is the container for thought. It structures meaning. Everything that we encounter in the theatre has form. The play has a form, the set has a form, the theatrical space has a form. The primary form and point of entry is the actor's body. The actor, Chekhov believed, needed to develop an acute sense of his own body, its native form, and its capacity to serve as a conduit for other forms.

FEELING OF BEAUTY AND FEELING FOR TRUTH

"Beauty is one of the outstanding qualities that distinguishes all works of art," says the preface to the Michael Chekhov book *On the Technique of Acting* (1991). Chekhov recognized that even ugliness could be beautiful, since for him beauty meant anything that was raw, organic, true, and coming from a wellspring of inner spiritual truthfulness. This idea ties in with one of his other core principles, **feeling for truth**.

In short, feeling for truth is the actor's ability to open himself to himself (his own inner psychology and motivations), his scene partner or partners, his audience and the script itself. Truth is hard to narrow down and define. Just as it is hard to understand a feeling of ease until you see and recognize its very noticeable opposite (a feeling of tension), it may be hard to pin down what a feeling of truth is, but we all have seen and experienced its polar opposite. We have all seen examples of stage falsehood and can recognize lack of truth immediately.

A FEELING OF THE WHOLE (ALSO CALLED A FEELING OF ENTIRETY)

A **feeling of the whole** can be seen in a few different ways. First there is the idea of the **ensemble**: that one actor is interdependent with his fellow actors and with the choreographer, the text coach, the lighting designer, the costume designer, the scenic designer, the director, and the list goes on and on. It takes a village to raise a child? Well, it takes two villages to put on a theatre production. Beyond that, the feeling of the whole is the idea that the whole work, assembled and created by all of these different people and components, has an overall feel. I recall seeing a theatre production with a friend in Boston. When I couldn't pinpoint why the production didn't work as a whole, despite some very compelling elements, my friend said, "It didn't work because there were no rules that consistently governed the world that they created." Chekhov understood this and advocated for an aesthetic consistency governing a work of theatre as a whole.

RADIATING/RECEIVING

Can you as an audience member sense when actors are giving you all of their energy? Can you sense when they are summoning up all of their spiritual and intellectual sustenance from within, harnessing it and delivering it across space to you in the audience? This is what Chekhov called **radiating**. Master Chekhov teacher Lenard Petit explains it best in *The Michael Chekhov Handbook for the Actor*:

> The inner work of acting, the knowledge, the feelings, the actions must in the end come out to touch the audience. Whatever is living within us can be sent out in an energetic wave. Radiating is an activity that will accompany an actor who is inspired. It can also come as a result of willing it. It produces pleasure for the actor to do and for the audience to witness. It simply is a sending out beyond the body what is alive within the body. It touches the audience because it actually goes out to them. (Petit 2009)

In addition to radiating, the actor also receives. Receiving is a way of harnessing energy from others, from the audience, from atmospheres; in short, from anything that exists around her. Think of it like a tractor beam gathering in all of the energy surrounding her and pulling it towards her, which in turn she can convert and radiate outward.

IMPROVISATION

For Chekhov, **improvisation** was not only for an initial exploration of the character, but a means of a final exploration once the character is built. Many times improvisation is the beginning stage, the point of entry for the actor who is just beginning to delve into a script and to find a way to get a handle on the character. Chekhov believed in this, but he also believed that improvisation at the final stages of character development formed a kind of "jewelry" in performance. This is a nice notion. Just as the outfit might be missing a little zazz until you pull that pair of rhinestone earrings out of the drawer, so too a performance might be just fine but lacking luster until the actor finds a little something extra through improvisation to put her performance on the next level. Chekhov advocated for improvisation through exploration of subtext or by rehearsing invented activities (Chekhov 1991). Through these kinds of improvised explorations, the actor could develop nuanced behavior in the character that might not otherwise be discovered.

FOCAL POINT

The **focal point** of a performance is exactly what it sounds like: it is the thing that the actor needs to highlight. In a play, a song, a work of art that unfolds over time, not every moment is of equal significance. Chekhov believed that it was the actor's job, with the help of a director, to find the most significant moments and highlight them for the audience. Whether the moments were spoken or communicated through movement or gesture, it was incumbent upon the actor to locate and highlight the focal points to ensure that those moments would appear distinct.

OBJECTIVE

Like his teacher Stanislavsky, Chekhov believed that the character needed to have a clearly defined goal on stage. He identified that the character has both an objective that serves the individual scene and a super-objective or overarching objective in the play.

Stanislavsky, Practical Aesthetics Technique, and all other action-based acting systems deal with the idea of objective. While the notion of the objective is always pretty much the same (what is the goal, what does my character want), the best way to construct and articulate the objective varies according to different practitioners. Michael Chekhov puts it like this: "Ideally, all objectives should begin with 'I want to . . .' followed by an 'actable' verb" (Chekhov 1991). This is a very simple, clear formula for defining the character's objective.

What Is It Like to Train with This Technique?

AN EXERCISE EXAMPLE

To try to give you an idea of what working with Michael Chekhov Technique might feel like, here is a sample exercise from the National Michael Chekhov Association. It is directed at exploring atmospheres and involves a technique called **Spy back.** When I was first exposed to this term, watching my fellow teaching artists who are Michael Chekhov practitioners, I found it strange. "Spy back" is an odd linguistic construction. To spy is to clandestinely observe something, and "back" asks the actor to look backwards in time. (The term probably sounded a lot cooler in Russian before it was translated. Everything sounds cooler in Russian.) But now that I get it, I like it!

The spy back allows the actor to reflect on and articulate her discoveries after the exercise or stage experience. Chekhov, who believed that intellectual processes actually kept the actor from being fully involved and truthfully engaged on stage, developed this technique in order to help actors temporarily set the intellect aside. Knowing that the "little intellect" (Petit 2009) will get its little say later allows the actor to be fully and entirely engaged in the moment in the imagination, body and impulse.

After you have finished a Michael Chekhov exercise, you will most likely be asked, in a group discussion, to "spy back" on the experience.

Atmospheres

Imagine various atmospheres as humans walking through them; select a brief mundane activity like tying your shoe or washing a dish. Repeat it, trying to keep your movements in harmony with the atmosphere. After each activity, spy back inwardly to determine how well your movements harmonized with the atmosphere and how did they differ from previous atmospheres.

Improvise the same atmospheres as molecules of energy using full body and voice. Remember, you are physicalizing an abstract idea, not a human one. Use every part of your body. Take turns with some people becoming humans who are permeated by the molecules of atmosphere. Return group to full humanity and re-imagine these atmospheres and repeat the sequence of activity ("tying your shoe"). Add a line of dialogue unrelated to the activity or sensation ("Hi, how are you?"). See if it is in greater harmony with the atmosphere now that you can more strongly imagine the gesture which lives invisibly around you.

ENSEMBLE

Chekhov work is all about ensemble. Michael Chekhov believed that the way a performance is developed in rehearsal is clearly present in the final production (Chekhov 1991). Actors needed to find a way of working together that would help to keep them open and connected to their environment and to each other.

Because of the emphasis on ensemble, you will find that Michael Chekhov training is truly an ensemble experience. Exercises are developed within a group environment. Although the actor pays careful attention to his individual process and discoveries, it is still very much within the context of the larger whole. The actor's work cannot help but be affected and informed by the people working around him. The actor also develops a sense of ease working toward these discoveries in tandem with his fellow actors.

THE FANS

The Michael Chekhov technique seems to resonate with any actor who wants to find a method for connecting with a play or script that is visceral rather than intellectual. If you are an actor who is stuck "in your head" (an overly analytical actor who can sometimes be paralyzed by your own thoughts and self-criticisms), Michael Chekhov Technique may be just the ticket.

As Michael Chekhov acting teacher David Meldman explained to me,

> Michael Chekhov's technique put the imaginative and fantastic qualities back into my acting, which had become staid, rigid, and overly intellectual. With Chekhov I can follow my instincts and characters wholly unique from each other. I am no longer trapped with only my own biography as a frame of reference. Our imagination gives us access to a nearly infinite number of lives, of skins to slip into. Chekhov's techniques help give us a direct access to that power, and to get ourselves out of our own way. The psycho-physical union experienced with psychological gesture wakes the whole self into a creative state.

THE CRITICS

Criticisms of Michael Chekhov's work seemed to have been more prevalent during his lifetime than today. The major objections to his work were political (his teaching, seen as being too mystical, was judged a threat to the Communist government in the early nineteen hundreds) and so powerful that he was forced to flee Russia in 1928 (National Michael Chekhov Association).

Today, Chekhov's work is highly respected and is even gaining popularity as a technique. The one drawback, some say, is that it is not an all-encompassing system and therefore cannot be substituted for a more comprehensive training like Stanislavsky's. It is not a panacea for all of acting's challenges, but neither is any other technique or system.

WHERE TO GO FOR MORE INFORMATION

One of the best resources out there is *The Michael Chekhov Handbook for the Actor*, by Lenard Petit. This guide not only explains Chekhov's ideas in a very accessible way, but provides clear exercises for the actor.

On the Technique of Acting and *Lessons for the Professional Actor* go into greater detail. Although they may be a little more cumbersome than the Petit book, they are a great way to get Chekhov's ideas fairly directly from the source.

Some of Chekhov's lectures are available under the title *On Theatre and the Art of Acting.*

For training in Chekhov Technique, check out the Michael Chekhov Acting Studio in New York (www.michaelchekhovactingstudio.com). Another good resource is the National Michael Chekhov Association (www.chekhov.net). The Michael Chekhov Association offers certification in Chekhov Technique (www.michaelchekhov.org/about-micha/teacher-training-certificate), as does a program through Kent State University (www.kent.edu/cde/summerprograms/michaelchekhov.cfm).

7

Meisner Technique

Acting is doing.—Sanford Meisner

There is a famous photograph of Sanford Meisner. In the photo he's wearing a big furry coat and appears to have Scotch tape on his glasses. Tape and furry coat aside, there is something deeply compelling about this picture, as if the true nature of the man Meisner is revealed through this image. His expression and his posture seem to communicate strength, intelligence, honesty, and integrity.

Another interesting characteristic of this image is repetition: everywhere you look for Meisner, this photograph appears. How fitting, since Meisner's work and philosophy of actor training all revolves around the idea of repetition. How appropriate, since in Meisner Technique repetition is the mechanism for the revelation of the honest and truthful self on stage.

How Meisner Technique Began

Sanford Meisner, like Stella Adler, was an actor in the Group Theatre. And, like Adler, Meisner took issue with director Lee Strasberg's overemphasis of emotional recall, which he found disruptive and disturbing. He wrote, "Actors are not guinea pigs to be manipulated, dissected, let alone in a purely negative way. Our approach was not organic, that is to say not healthy" (Mestnik 2011).

Meisner also felt a disturbing sense of disconnection between actors in the American theatre. The techniques in use in the Group Theatre, he believed, pulled the actor deeper and deeper into self and further and further away from her scene partner and the action of the moment. After many conversations with Adler and fellow Group Theatre actor Harold Clurman, Meisner decided that American actors could not create theatre that was truthful and honest simply by replicating (and thereby misinterpreting and corrupting) Russian principles. An American approach needed to be developed, one that honored Stanislavsky's principles but was also uniquely American.

BASIC PRINCIPLES

While Strasberg's emphasis on emotional recall required that the actor draw on personal emotional experience from the past to give life to a character on stage, Meisner instead sought ways for the actor to harness the power of imagination, rather than actual experience, to create the character's stage life.

Meisner believed that acting that was specific and truthful could only come out the actor's genuine response to circumstances and other people. Therefore, his training method accessed the actor's impulses, through exercises that demanded responses and genuine behavior in the moment. The core of Meisner's training technique involves repetition. Meisner believed that through repetition, the actor would learn how to place his focus on his scene partner and devote all of his energy to connecting in the moment to the partner on stage. Repetition would teach the actor to respond viscerally, rather than intellectually, to his scene partner. It would train him to work instinctively and impulsively without premeditation.

How Repetition Exercises Work

1. Objective repetition without changes

In the beginning, a simple phrase is repeated between two scene partners. The phrase is usually a simple observation. It is the first thing that the actor notices about the other person. It can be an observation of what she sees. For example, one actor might say to the other actor, "You are wearing a blue shirt," and the other actor will reply, "I am wearing a blue shirt." This phrase is repeated by each actor over and over again. Through the process of repetition, some ingredient will change organically; the vocal inflection or dynamic of the phrase might change. The partners must simply concentrate on one another, following the flow of the phrase and responding organically to its subtle shift in nature. This kind of repetition exercise is designed to teach the actor:

- How to notice and allow for impulses by commenting on the first thing that she notices. The exercise allows the freedom to abandon politeness. If the first thing that the actor notices in the other actor is "You're having a bad hair day today," she is free to express it without self-censorship. As Meisner teacher Elizabeth Mestnik describes training actors in Meisner technique, "We are developing their ability to act from an impulse rather than their intellect, responding from the heart, not the head. Just repeating also removes the need to come up with the words, which helps keeps the student from thinking too much" (Mestnik 2011).

- How to put her entire focus on the scene partner and behavior. The actor is able to channel her energy entirely toward the other actor, taking the focus off of herself, removing the pressure to be clever or creative and interesting, and allowing her to focus on nothing but her connection to the other person.

- How to reveal her true feelings in the moment without fear. If the actor is fully present with her partner in the moment, her true feelings may bubble to the surface. By the simple act of repeating without thought, true emotion may come forth without the actor having time to judge or censor herself.

2. Repetition with changes

The next phase of repetition allows the actor to alter the phrase that is being repeated. The change must arise from a true organic response rather than from an intellectual idea. The actor must change the phrase instinctively by reacting to information from his scene partner. If the phrase being repeated started out as something like "You are wearing a blue shirt," but along the way the phrase changed intonation and inflection through repetition, the other actor's organic response in time might include an instinctual perception that causes him to morph the phrase into "You don't like it." This phrase is repeated by both partners until it organically morphs and changes again.

When I studied Meisner years ago, I was always getting into trouble with the instructor during this phase of the exercise. I would repeat and repeat, as expected, but when it came to altering the phrase, I was a bad actor in Meisnerland. At the time I was bewildered that I was constantly asked to stop the exercise and start over. It is only now, years later, that I understand why. I did not change the phrase when I was truly inspired to do so. I changed the phrase because I felt that the exercise was becoming uninteresting to anyone who was watching—that I was not being clever enough or entertaining enough. This is the exact opposite of Meisner's intention for actors. Meisner intended for the actor to change the repetition when and only when his partner inspires him organically to do so. Change comes from impulse, not from premeditation or cognition. Meisner's goal was to get the actor out of her head. I was going through Meisner's steps while staying stuck in my head. Meisner's objective was total focus on the scene partner, but I was focused on myself and my audience (in this case, my fellow classmates' response to my work).

Repetition with changes, when done organically, allows the actor:

- To focus on observation. The actor not only hones the skill of observation but states the observed behavior without self-censorship. The result is observation that is raw and truthful, rather than polite and restricted.

- To work from impulse, rather than from intellect. If the phrase changes as the result of intellectual intervention (as it did when I was a young, misguided actor doing the exercise), it will be readily apparent that the actor is trying to control the outcome rather than living truthfully in the moment.

3. Subjective repetition with changes

In the first step of repetition, the actor made a simple statement of observation about the other person. This statement had no value judgment. It expressed no particular point of view or perspective. Now, in this third step in repetition, the actor states an opinion or voices a point of view about what he observes. Whatever the actor notices, he must speak from truth. He must not sugarcoat, extrapolate, consider feelings or consequences; he must simply say what comes to mind. This could be a statement such as "You look tense today," repeated as "I look tense today," or "You look like you're going to cry." Whatever the observed behavior or immediate response, it must be truthful.

How can you do this and be a civilized person? As the actor I might notice and state, "You have an enormous zit on your forehead" (repeated as "I have an enormous zit on my forehead"). Certainly these kinds of statements, truthful or not, do not win friends and influence people. As Meisner says in the book *Sanford Meisner on Acting* (1987), "You try to be logical, as in life. You try to be polite, as in life. May I say, as the world's oldest living teacher, 'Fuck polite!' . . . You have one thing to do, and that is to pick up the repetition from your partner. . . . You cannot be a gentleman and be an actor."

What is the value of this, you might ask?

I currently have a strange epidemic in my classroom: too-polite actors. A young woman jumps to my mind. She is very capable and naturally gifted as an actor, but she is so afraid in her scene work of being impolite, too aggressive or unladylike, that she is stuck in every scene that she does. Nothing happens. Scene work for her is a steady stream of squished impulses. You can watch brilliant ideas flicker across her face that are censored, then extinguished, and die. I have to chase her around the room and scream at her to stop being polite until I fluster and enrage her so much that when she returns to the scene, something happens and her scene partner gets her true, uncensored response. If she did some Meisner training, it would save me wear and tear on my new sneakers.

In some cases though, what is honestly felt and observed is not hurtful, prickly, overbearing, or coarse; it is sweet and touching. Here is a lovely example, again from master Meisner teacher Elizabeth Mestnik (2011):

> I once had a young man say to a really beautiful young woman, "You are gorgeous." It was completely truthful and heartfelt, and this beautiful young woman was so completely overwhelmed by the honesty and genuineness that she welled up with tears. Why? Because the safe space of the classroom allowed her to let go of her defenses and show her feelings, and because we don't get opportunities for this sincerity very often in real life! But I say in this work we are not looking to behave as we would in real life—we want to be more truthful than we are in real life. That is why audiences pay money to see us, because we will reveal to them something beyond what they experience in the everyday.

This is such a beautiful example of what can be achieved through Meisner repetition: a complete revelation of the true self and organic thought. In daily life, this young man probably would not have revealed his honest and genuine thoughts about the other actor. The exercise allowed him to be completely truthful, spontaneously in the moment, without intellectualizing, controlling, or editing his thoughts.

The final phase of repetition allows the actor:

- To continue to work from instinct
- To stay fully connected with the scene partner
- To speak from a standpoint of emotional, organic truth rather than from intellectual control

THE ACTION IS THE ACTIVITY

We can see from the repetition exercises that Meisner is all about being truthful. The actor must, in short, stop acting. The only road to truth on stage is to stop thinking and to start doing, and in the doing to do what is honest.

Meisner's method focuses on commitment to the character's objective. Character, Meisner believed, is created by wanting and longing. To become the character, the actor must understand what the character needs. One cannot become Hamlet without understanding his all-consuming need to avenge his father's murder. The objective creates the character.

To aid the actor in this discovery, Meisner developed a new phase of training: the **independent activity**. In the independent activity the actor must take on a task that requires his entire concentration. The action that the actor chooses must be difficult to achieve and must have an end goal that can be completed. Additionally, the actor must have an objective; that is, a singular reason for completing this task. Examples of tasks that meet this criterion might be

- Untangling a knot of gold necklaces because the actor borrowed one of the necklaces from her roommate without asking, and must return them to her jewelry box before she returns home
- Removing a sticky cheesecake from a pan in one piece so that the actor can present it to his girlfriend for her birthday
- Knitting a scarf to give to the actor's grandmother for Christmas

As you can see from the above tasks, there is a different degree of urgency involved with each. Task one seems fairly urgent, task two could be slightly less urgent, and, depending on how far away the Christmas season is or how old Grandma is, task three might have very little urgency. It is up to the actor to decide on the degree of urgency involved in completing the task.

While the actor is fully engaged with executing this task, her scene partner will begin the repetition exercise. This dictates that the actor involved with the task be fully engaged with the task and truthfully engaged with her partner.

This may sound simple, but it is difficult. The first time I had to do this, I chose the unfortunate task of completing a crossword puzzle. I wish I had known how to knit. Having an engaging task that was language-dependent while I was repeating with my partner nearly made my head explode. The temptation, as you can well imagine, is to shut out the partner so that you can complete the activity. The more all-enveloping the task (like my crossword puzzle), the greater the temptation is to do this. The challenge for the actor is to do both things: to complete the task and to communicate through repetition with the scene partner.

What is the value of this?

Well, if you've ever had a roommate, girlfriend, husband, parent, cat, dog, or ferret interrupt you with chatter while you were paying your bills, you know. Interruptions create tension. The need to complete a task creates tension. Having your attention pulled in two different directions creates tension. Theatre is all about tension between people.

The independent activity creates a situation under which conflict between two people cannot help but arise. Because the actor has already laid a foundation for responding organically and truthfully to stimuli from his partner by doing the repetition exercises, in the conflict that may naturally arise through the engagement in the activity, his response will be uncensored and truthful. Through full engagement with the chosen task and with the scene partner, the real emotion that the actor is feeling will surface (rather than a manufactured emotion driven by emotional recall).

We have seen this notion time and again through those acting practitioners who have chosen to separate themselves from Strasberg and the Method: acting is not about feeling; acting is about doing. Emotion is not something that is to be conjured up in and of itself to serve the scene; emotion surfaces as the result of pursuing action on stage.

EMOTIONAL PREPARATION

While Meisner balked at Strasberg's use of emotional recall, he does acknowledge that the actor must come on stage with an already full emotional life. He terms this **preparation**.

> Before the scene begins, through your imagination—maybe by daydreaming, or however you go about it—you get yourself ticking emotionally, so that when you enter the scene you have an emotional fullness which lasts as long as the first moment. It may or may not come up again in the course of the scene, but it brings you on alive and full. (Meisner 1987)

On the topic of preparation, Meisner is somewhat obtuse. He does not prescribe a way for the actor to come onto the stage in a believable state; he only states its necessity and that it is up to the individual actor to determine how to get there. Basically, it's an I-don't-care-how-you-do-it-but-you-need-to-find-a-way thing. I find this aspect slightly problematic. To state that it is a personal choice how the actor gets to this state of emotional reality without providing a tool to generate it is puzzling. Without guidance, actors may find themselves falling back on emotional recall, which Meisner railed against, in the effort to create an emotional reality on stage.

MOVING PAST REPETITION

It should be noted that repetition is the foundation of the house in Meisner training, but is not the house itself. Through repetition exercises and the many variations and steps that follow, the actor builds a foundation of listening, responding in the moment, utilizing impulse rather than intellect, and organically finding truth in conflict. Once impulse is opened through repetitious dialogue, actors begin to be called upon through Meisner's work to think more like actors. At a certain point, having learned the lessons afforded by repetition, the actor leaves it behind in favor of a true dialogue. As Meisner himself explained,

> In the beginning the mindless repetition of the basic exercise had value.
> It eliminated a need for you to think. . . . Now I'm saying we have moved
> beyond the fundamental. Now it is possible to respond reasonably. So if
> your partner asks you what time it is, for God's sake look at your watch
> and tell him! (Meisner 1987)

After repetition has helped him to get out of his own head and
enabled him to interact more truthfully and spontaneously with his
scene partner, the actor becomes free to respond organically without
repetition. Improvising a scene provides a wonderful bridge between
repetition exercises and working with an actual script. Having found
truthful interaction through improvisation, the actor can now move on
to the words of the playwright with a greater degree of truth.

Whether it is through improvisation or an actual play, the actor,
as a result of the foundational training, should retain the essential
ideas: everything that the actor does is in response to their partner,
from one moment to another. Everything that the actor does on stage
is impulse given life. The actor has a unique voice that is truthful and
honest. Through the imagination and through the pursuit of objective, the actor brings unique life to the character. As Meisner said,
"Anybody can *read*. But acting is *living* under imaginary circumstances" (1987).

What's It Like to Train Under This System?

Meisner training can be bewildering at first. Listening and repeating is
a strange experience. I must say in my first stab at Meisner I was one of
the many actors who just plain old didn't get it. This was, in my case,
a combination of youth, impatience, and a bad teacher.

That said, in the hands of the right teacher and with the right frame
of mind for the actor, Meisner can be an invaluable tool. If you are that
too-polite actor who censors instinct for the sake of decorum, if you
are the actor who is trapped in your head and over-thinks everything,

or if you are the actor who plans what you will do next instead of listening, Meisner might be just the tool that you need.

AN EXPERIENCE

I usually end each of these sections representing the critics and the fans of a given technique. Here I want to give you a very personal response from my colleague, Marisa Guida. As I think you can see from her thoughts, the critics of Meisner are no doubt those who do not have an experience, for whatever reason, where they are able to fully commit to the training. A successful Meisner experience seems to require that wonderful alchemy of a good teacher, an open partner, and being in an open and receptive place in one's own life.

I believe for any method or technique to work, one must drink the juice. All of it. No little baby sips. You have to chug every last drop or you are just wasting your time. Drinking the juice is equal to giving 100,000,000 percent of your body, mind, and soul. Your intelligence, wit, and talent are of little to no use for the efficacy of certain exercises. For example, one of the first, the best, and the most famous Meisner exercises is repetition.

Repetition can be exhausting if you are partnered with someone who refuses to drink the juice. On the inverse, when two people really let go of the [stuff] they think is awesome and just allow themselves to be, and see and hear the other person they are working with, that one exercise can change the way you go through life. How many times have you asked someone, "How are you doing?" and they answer you, "Fine, how are you?" and you answer, "Good, thanks." And then walk away.

Humans and life are too complex to be "fine" and "good"—but we say that, all the time. We say it—but if the person asking was really listening, they might hear the truth through the lies. Repetition pulls the truth out in the open. In day-to-day situations truly expressing our emotions, thoughts, and feelings is not always socially acceptable. So we lock them up. An actor does not have the luxury of ignoring everyone around her or shutting down her emotions.

I remember some of my first experiences with repetition. I so badly wanted to improvise and tried to be clever and funny and move on from anything mundane. And I would hear "Repeat!!!" being screamed at me from across the room. When it clicked and I just let go and would listen and repeat, I heard and felt and shared more than ever before.

People get frustrated with repetition because it's repetitious. This exercise requires the same things as a successful career in acting: a great deal of discipline, patience, and focus.

I remember being pushed beyond my limits of comfort. Only the truth was acceptable; there was no armor to hide behind.

I drank the juice. I gave as much as I knew how to give at that time. After living more of this thing called life, I can only imagine the unbelievable things I would discover revisiting the work.

WHERE TO GO FOR MORE INFORMATION

A wonderful place to start is with the book *Sanford Meisner on Acting*, written by Sanford Meisner and Dennis Longwell. The books of Larry Silverberg are also helpful. Each of the three workbooks in his series entitled *The Sanford Meisner Approach* tackles a different area of the technique.

Although these books are all a wonderful way to gain a deeper understanding of Meisner technique, nothing beats on-your-feet experience with a trained teacher. The Neighborhood Playhouse, where it all began, is still alive and well and offers a Certificate in Acting (neighborhoodplayhouse.org). In addition to Meisner training, the program offers training in voice and speech, dance, Alexander Technique, and singing. It is structured very much like a traditional MFA (although it grants the certificate rather than the terminal degree).

Other options include the William Esper Studio (esperstudio.com) and the Gately/Poole Conservatory (gatelypooleacting.com). Meisner training abounds with many classes available in many different areas. Choose wisely. Know the difference for yourself between the frustration of growth in your craft and the frustration of a bad teacher. If it feels right, it is right. If it feels wrong, it is wrong.

Trust your instincts. That's what Sanford Meisner would have wanted.

8

Stella Adler

You have to get beyond your own precious inner experiences. The actor cannot afford to look only to his own life for all his material nor pull strictly from his own experience to find his acting choices and feelings. The ideas of the great playwrights are almost always larger than the experiences of even the best actors.

—STELLA ADLER

Who Was Stella Adler?

In everything that has been written about Stella Adler, one comes away with the sense that she was loving, committed to truth, ferociously smart and independent, passionate about the craft of acting, and a force to be reckoned with. Born in 1901, Adler spent her entire life acting and teaching and is still considered to be one of the most influential teachers of theatre. Her students and the followers of her technique are famous and legendary: Robert De Niro, Warren Beatty, Candice Bergen, and, most notably, her student and friend Marlon Brando. A successful and highly acclaimed actor, Adler always sought to improve her craft, never satisfied with standing still as an artist. In her lifetime career, Adler proved that she was just as committed to teaching her craft as she was to practicing it.

Born to parents in the Yiddish theatre, the actors Jacob and Sara Adler, Stella Adler began acting at the age of four. She was widely acclaimed in the Yiddish theatre, but sought more mainstream roles and eventually made her way to Broadway.

Adler was one of the original members of the Group Theatre, which we mentioned in the chapter on Lee Strasberg. To understand a little more about Adler, let's revisit the Group Theatre and its ideals.

The Group Theatre, you'll remember from our discussion about Lee Strasberg and the Method, was founded by Harold Clurman, Cheryl Crawford, and Lee Strasberg. Dissatisfied with what they felt was the shallow and socially irrelevant nature of the theatre that was prevalent at the end of the 1920s, the group created a permanent theatre ensemble as a way of shining a light on the important issues of their times (American Masters 1997). They sought to create a new and politically influential kind of theatre that would showcase original American plays. Modeling their approach on that of the Moscow Art Theatre, they founded a collaborative ensemble rather than promoting individual performers. Their communal ideas were certainly more in line with Russian aesthetics than with existing American principles (these ideas and the political charge of their work later caused some members to be investigated by the House Un-American Activities Committee to investigate possible ties to Communism). The Group Theatre brought a new level of realism and relevance to the American theatre and may have been the most influential theatre in America in the twentieth century.

Although Adler was a featured actor in the Group Theatre and was invited to be a founding member, she was certainly not in agreement with all of their ideas and principles. She seems to have had reservations from the get-go, including concern about the Group's politics and qualms about the artistic teachings of founding member Lee Strasberg.

Prior to working with the Group Theatre, Adler had joined the American Laboratory, run by actors Richard Boleslawski and Maria Ouspenskaya. Boleslawki and Ouspenskaya had both been members of the Moscow Art Theatre. No doubt training with these actors formed the foundation for Adler's thinking about the theatre even before she joined the Group

Theatre. In the early 1930s Adler took a temporary leave from the Group Theatre to study with Stanislavsky in Europe.

In our discussion of the Method, we presented Adler's meeting with Stanislavsky and the resulting schism that it caused in the Group Theatre in a way that painted Adler as the chief perpetrator of miscommunication and misunderstanding. Perhaps here we can get a bit closer to her perspective on the situation. Without having been there, we will never know how it all truly occurred . . .

Going Her Own Way: A Break with Lee Strasberg and the Method

Stella Adler was one of the very few American actors to study directly with Konstantin Stanislavsky. During her time with the Group Theatre, Adler had been resistant, you will remember, to the process of emotional recall, finding it dangerous and intrusive. The psychological destructiveness of this part of the craft, as articulated by Strasberg, marred her joy in performing. Adler once remarked, "Drawing on the emotions I experienced, for example, when my mother died to create a role is sick and schizophrenic. If that is acting, I don't want to do it!" (Beginners Guide to Acting).

While studying with Stanislavsky, Adler came to believe that Lee Strasberg's focus on affective memory was something of a departure and misinterpretation of Stanislavsky's current ideas. She returned from studying with Stanislavsky wishing to share all that she had learned or interpreted, and explained her new understanding of his teachings at the Group Theatre. Many members of the Group, it seems, received these teachings enthusiastically, but it is said by many that this split between Adler's ideas and Lee Strasberg's ideas formed the schism in the Group that ultimately led to its unraveling.

Adler went on to open her own acting studio to promote the teachings of Stanislavsky as she understood them. The Stella Adler Theatre Studio (the name under which it opened in the mid-1940s) was later renamed the Stella Adler Conservatory of Acting, and now operates as the Stella Adler Studio of Acting. The school is still thriving in New York with a second school opened in Los Angeles.

Basic Principles

THE IMAGINATION, NOT EMOTION OR EXPERIENCE

Lee Strasberg believed that Stanislavsky's system dictated that the actor delve deeply into his own emotional experiences. By reliving past sensations and feelings, the actor could then re-create and replicate them on stage. Conversely, Stella Adler believed that an actor's talent lay within his imaginative power. Using past experience and drawing on past life circumstances, Adler felt, was a shortcut for the actor; it was a kind of acting laziness. It was imagination, not experience, that was important. For Adler, imagination formed the foundation of acting craft.

The Stella Adler Studio has this quote from Adler on its current training website:

> Drama depends on doing, not feeling; feeling is a by-product of doing. Our approach to acting depends on connecting strongly to each other by way of actions and creating dramatic events that take place between "I and thou," not between "me and myself." These actions include the subtle, creative, onstage choices to which actors commit.

Rather than relive and re-create emotional memories that would replicate emotional experience on stage, Adler felt that the actor should create anew, building a reality step by step by specifically envisioning the character in an environment and in a set of given circumstances. It is the actor's supreme commitment to doing something in a specific time and place that generates an emotional response, rather than the effort to generate an emotional response in and of itself. The actor's task is to create reality from words on paper by fleshing them out using her own creativity.

HOW TO BEGIN TO CREATE A REALITY THAT THE ACTOR CAN "BUY INTO"

Where Am I?

To create truth on stage, the actor needs to use his imaginative power to create a world and set of circumstances that he can believe in and invest in. But how does the actor begin?

Much like a detective, the actor begins by asking himself questions. One of the first questions to be asked is: "Where am I?"

Everybody's gotta be somewhere! That is to say, all action occurs in a specific time and place. The nature of that time and place changes behavior (for example, we behave differently in a museum or a library than we do in a shopping mall or in our own home). Asking the question "Where am I?" and answering it with specificity is the first step to creating a believable reality.

Action: What Must Be Done?

One of the next questions to be answered is "What must be done/accomplished in this place that I am in?"

An action, as our friend Stanislavsky put it, is something that one does. The character, functioning in a specific time and place, has a specific task that must be accomplished. It may be as simple as finding a key so that the door can be opened, or something far more complex (such as getting an enemy to sign over an estate). At every given moment in a play a character is "doing" something. It is these individual units of "doing" that make up the play.

How Do I Do It?

How a character does something in a play—that is, how he performs an action under a specific set of circumstances—uncovers the meaning of the play. A physical action will be performed differently in different circumstances. A simple action like finding a key to open a door changes depending on the circumstances surrounding that action. A character who is sneaking inside late at night will perform the action of searching for the key very differently from a character who is searching for the key to open the door while being chased by a murderer. The way that actions are performed creates story, meaning, and character.

How Do I Find an Action?

To know what one is "doing" on stage, the actor must ask herself these questions:

- Who am I?
- Who am I talking to?
- How am I trying to make that person feel?
- How am I going to try to do what I need to get done?

As we saw in an earlier quote of Adler's, dramatic events "take place between 'I and thou,' not between 'me and myself.'" Dramatic action happens between characters on stage, rather than being born of self-reflection and inner recollection. Because dramatic action is an exchange of energy on stage between characters, *who* you are talking to and determining what you want from them and how you need to make them feel in order to accomplish that are vitally important questions to ask.

Once the actor can answer those questions specifically, he can then ask himself:

- What will I do when I do or don't get it?

If action is all about "doing" on stage, we either get done what we need to get done, or we don't. We either find the keys to open the door or we do not. We either convince the person to sign over the estate or we do not. How we respond to that winning or losing and what we choose to do next is what reveals character and propels the story forward.

THE PLAY IS NOT IN THE WORDS

Hamlet once said, "The play's the thing (wherein I'll catch the conscience of the king)."

For Adler, the play is *not* the thing! The *actor* is the thing.

The play—the story of the play and its characters—is not contained within the text. The text is a framework that needs fleshing out. It is the actors and their specific imaginative choices that make the play.

> When an actor first approaches a play, the script is an alien thing. Woven of words not of his choosing, peopled with strangers, marked with events he has nor experienced and situations he has not explored, the play stands all in shadow. The actor infuses the play with the light of life. Reading the words of a play, the actor systematically works backward from the words to the sources of the play and then works forward to speak the words—simply and meaningfully. It is a creative research process, to find what he can use to fill the text with as much insight, thought, and imagination as was stirring in the playwright before he arrived at the result of all his labor—the result being: the words. (Rotté 2000)

Plays do not hold meaning until the actor *gives* the text meaning through the imagination. This is the antithesis of David Mamet and Practical Aesthetics Technique, which maintains that everything needed to communicate story and character is provided in the text specifically by the playwright.

Adler claims the exact opposite: that words themselves are empty things and that it is the job of the actor to fill them. Maintaining that words often mean something other than their literal meaning, she held that theatre is what happens behind the the surface of the words (Rotté 2000).

To know what one is "saying" on stage, which is part and parcel of what one is "doing" on stage, the actor must ask himself these questions:

What am I actually saying?

And, perhaps most importantly,

How can I put what I'm saying into my own words?

Getting to the core of what words and actions mean to the actor on a specific and personal level, the actor can create an inhabitable and truthful reality for herself and the audience.

What's It Like to Train Under This System?

THE CRITICS

The most obvious and vocal critics of Adler's work emerged at the time that the Group Theatre was splintering: as Adler rejected Strasberg's interpretations of Stanislavsky's work, Strasberg's fans rejected her rejection. Her work clearly polarized the theatre training community at the time. No doubt, after many decades, some small vestiges of the resentment of Adler's views remains among practitioners of Strasberg's Method.

THE FANS

Stella Adler's fans are many. Her work is widely seen as an important next step in bringing Stanislavsky's ideas to America. It was not only her interpretation and understanding of Stanislavsky's work at its source that distinguished her, but her holistic view of the actor and the actor's craft. For Stella Adler, one could not grow as an actor without growing as a human being. Adler herself was a ferociously independent, free-thinking person, so it is no surprise that she believed that it was essential that all actors bring their own point of view and intellect to their work. Passionate though she was, she was eclectic in her approach to the craft of acting and did not believe that there was any one right way. Like Stanislavsky, her "system" was not a system; it was a series of tools that the actor could use in service of bringing a script to life formed the framework for how the tools, training, and discipline were delivered.

One of Adler's most famous sayings (popping up just about everywhere you can read about her) is this: "Your talent is in your choice."

What does this mean?

It means that talent grows from the ability to make distinctive and specific choices based on individual ideas. As actors we make many tiny choices from moment to moment as we fulfill the intentions of a play and a given text. It is these choices that create the play and its inhabitants. We choose, as actors, what we create.

But more than that, it is the actor's choice to determine his own level of commitment to the craft of acting. Adler believed that the study of acting was a lifetime commitment to training the voice, the body, the intellect, the imagination, and the spirit. It was the actor's choice to determine that level of commitment—and not just the commitment to training and craft—but the ongoing investigation into the body, the mind, the soul, and what it means to be human. In her own life, Adler always chose to fully engage her talent, not only as an artist, but as a thinking and feeling human being. It is this choice that made her work so great.

WHERE TO GO FOR MORE INFORMATION

There have been many books written by and about Stella Adler. Two great places to start are *The Technique of Acting* and *The Art of Acting*.

Training is available at the Stella Adler Studio of Acting, with locations in New York and Los Angeles (www.stellaadler.com and www.stellaadler-la.com). Part-time and summer workshops are available, as are a three-year conservatory program that grants a certificate upon completion, and BFA program offered through New York University.

Uta Hagen

Nobody ever learns how [to act]. The search for human behavior is infinite. You'll never understand it all. I think that's wonderful. —UTA HAGEN

If you took the very best that Method acting had to offer and put it in a blender with the very best elements of action-based acting systems, you'd wind up with Uta Hagen.

Sounds like some pretty powerful stuff? That's because Uta Hagen was a pretty powerful lady.

Uta Hagen was a great actor, acting teacher, and student of the human being. Born in Germany, she began acting professionally at the age of eighteen. She debuted in 1938 as Shakespeare's Ophelia, made the leap to Broadway a year later in Chekhov's *The Seagull,* and went on to appear in twenty-two Broadway productions, including originating the role of Martha in Edward Albee's *Who's Afraid of Virginia Woolf.* Critics and playwrights alike hailed her performances as compelling and truthful, yet her work was always growing and changing. She learned from her own mistakes and developed a technique for herself that would always keep her performances fresh and vibrant. Then she made it her mission to teach other actors the techniques that she had developed. She began teaching at the acting school HB Studios in 1945 (later marrying the studio's founder, Herbert Berghof) and spent the rest of her career teaching a new generation of actors her techniques.

Hagen's commitment to teaching eventually surpassed her commitment to her own acting career. As actor Jack Lemmon wrote,

> This extraordinary woman is one of the greatest actresses I have seen in my lifetime, yet Uta Hagen has deliberately made her acting career secondary to teaching and directing others so that they might benefit. Lord knows what exalted position she might have attained had she chosen to concentrate on her own acting career, but I guarantee that she has absolutely no regrets. Nor should she, because Uta Hagen has given so much to so many. (Jason Bennett Actor's Workshop)

Basic Principles

In the 1950s acting often had a kind of artificial, untruthful quality to it. Audiences accepted a kind of superficial behavior in actors. Actors "played at" being the character, capturing easy surface qualities rather than truly inhabiting the character and creating a dimensional and realistic human being. In response to this, Hagen developed acting methods that were designed to help actors to *become* the character, rather than to simply *be like* the character. She believed that it was essential that the actor use his authentic self and life experience to create character; that character arose not from a source external to the actor, but from within his own personality. For Hagen, the study of acting was the study of the human being and what it means to be human. And the art of acting required a driving need to communicate as well as the discipline and imagination to make that communication effective.

In addition to life experience and personal connection to a character, Hagen believed in the power of research. She asked her actors to research everything about their characters' social and physical world, and to flesh out a detailed biography of the character in order to create a believable inner life and an authentic performance.

Authentic behavior on stage, she believed, also depended upon the actor's commitment to action. Hagen maintained that in life, people were always engaged in doing things; they were never idle. If a person were waiting for a train, for example, Hagen said, he could do many things—he could talk to himself, he could fiddle with change, he could watch others—but even while waiting people are always engaged in action.

This leads us to another one of Hagen's core beliefs: the importance of the physical senses when creating theatre. Work with the actor's five senses—touch, smell, taste, sight, and sound—was vital as a gateway to truthful behavior. If the actor could not sense the character's surroundings viscerally, in Hagen's view, the performance could not be truthful.

HAGEN'S BOOKS

What do Uta Hagen and Konastantin Stanislavsky have in common?

(No, this is not the setup to a bad joke.) Both Hagen and Stanislavsky became dissatisfied with their earlier work, generated new work, and disassociated themselves from their previous notions.

To my way of thinking this is an incredibly brave and noble thing to do. It is natural to become dissatisfied with our work when it is not well received or deemed successful in the eyes of the public; it is far more unusual to reconsider our approach when we have been *successful*. Both Hagen and Stanislavsky found a wide and appreciative audience for their work. Both became dissatisfied with their success because of the way their work was being interpreted and applied. Both strived to create something more authentic and useful. Both succeeded.

In 1953 Uta Hagen wrote the book *Respect for Acting*. It received great acclaim and was used in actor training everywhere. It was viewed as *the* textbook for acting students. Yet Hagen became gravely disappointed with the results of her book's popularity. She felt that young actors took away the wrong ideas from her book and brought those ideas to the stage, often with disastrous results. It seemed that her call for truthful acting had led actors too close to presenting daily life in performance. Under-energized and disengaged on stage, they had achieved casualness in the pursuit of truth (Bartow 2006).

Hagen's dissatisfaction with the results of *Respect for Acting* led her to create *A Challenge for the Actor*. This second book changed and modified some of the terminology that she had used in her earlier book. More importantly, the new book attempted to lay out more clearly how to use self to create an authentic performance while at the same time making a distinction between acting truthfully onstage and behaving truthfully in life. Hagen wanted her actors to realize that art is larger than life; it is a heightened reality, not reality itself. Thus she hoped to correct a misunderstanding she believed to be the chief flaw in her earlier work.

In her ongoing commitment to actor training and to finding new ways of reaching and communicating with actors, Hagen released the video *Uta Hagen's Acting Class*, a view into her master acting classes, in 2001. An enormous gift to the profession, this two-part video is as close as the modern actor can come to being trained by Hagen herself, in all of her articulate, succinct, chain-smoking glory.

Hagen also wrote a cookbook in 1976, entitled *Love for Cooking*. I don't think that this book had much of an effect on actors. Maybe it made a select few of them fat.

SIX STEPS

It seems that the more we look at various training methodologies, the more we can see patterns emerge. Most great theatre thinkers try very hard to break things down for the actor; they try to create guideposts and an identifiable series of steps to help the actor to approach their work. It is the best way to make something unknowable knowable, and to make the subjective and the complex something that can be handled and mastered.

Uta Hagen was no different. She created six steps to help the actor to uncover and discover the world of any play that she encounters. Here they are.

Step #1: Who Am I?

The actor must start with this basic question. To answer this question, the actor needs to determine:

- **What is my present state of being?** That is to say, what is happening in my (the character's) life right now that is generating a particular kind of energy? Stanislavsky spoke of the character's tempo-rhythm, an inner pace that dictated the speed and intensity of their outer behavior. This is a very similar idea. In this Hagen's approach, the character's rhythm and energy are driven by her current circumstances and their effect on her.

- **How do I perceive myself?** The way a character perceives himself may or may not be true and in line with the way that other characters in the play perceive him. A character may feel like a
victim while others see him as a bully. A character may imagine that he is a great success while others see him as a huge failure. Hagen stresses that perception of self is a temporary state for the character, that it is fluid and may change quickly.

- **What am I wearing?** What a character is wearing is dictated by many factors. Self-esteem and self-perception influence what a character wears. Environment and time period also affect clothing. A character may wear a ski jacket on a cold winter day or a rain boots on a rainy day. Clothing may also give information about the character's time period and social status. Understanding what the character is wearing on the outside provides very specific information about her psychology and environment.

Step #2: What Are the Circumstances?

- **What time is it?** We can look at this question on both a micro and a macro level. Time can be about the hour, the day, the season, or the year, or it can be viewed on a greater level. Instead of looking at time in the small and immediate sense, we can instead look at the time period in history and how that time period influences social behavior and perceptions. Working with a character from a very different time period than the actor's necessitates a great deal of research.

- **At what time does my selected life begin?** This is a strange and unusual question that no one but Hagen has thought to ask: when, exactly, is the moment that my life, as the character, begins in the play? The character's selected life may begin as soon as he is mentioned by another character on stage, or it may begin with his first entrance.

- **What surrounds me?** This question addresses the immediate landscape, the weather, and the nature of the objects in the environment where the character is in the scene.

- **Where am I?** Environment is a vital part of Hagen's work, requiring full use of the actor's senses. Environment affects behavior. People do not behave the same way in a museum as they would in a ballpark. Place affects character. Creating a specific environment for your character to inhabit will help you to create a believable world to be in.

- **What are the immediate circumstances?** What has just happened or is happening to the character? What does the character expect or plan to happen next and to happen later on? Hagen believed that the character's present must have an immediate and detailed past. This idea may be familiar to many actors as the **moment before** or what Stanislavsky termed the **mantle**. The preceding circumstances must be clearly identified by the actor in order to make the character's present believable.

Step #3: What Are My Relationships?
How do I stand in relationship to the circumstances, the place, the objects, and the other people related to my circumstances?

When we hear the word "relationships," most of us automatically think about our relationships to *people*. It is vital for the actor to explore the nature of her relationship to the other characters in the play (both those on stage and those who are mentioned but may never appear in the play), but characters also have an equally powerful relationship to environment, objects, and life circumstances. The character's circumstances and her understanding of them greatly affect her self-perception. What is going on in the character's world may make her feel frightened, angry, or elated. The way the character interacts with objects affects and shapes all aspects of behavior.

Step #4: What Do I Want?
What is my main objective?

What is my immediate need or goal? What is my goal in the play? Or I may ask, what is my goal in the scene or my goal at any given moment? What do I want from the other character or characters on stage? Without knowing what the character wants there is no action; there will be no driving force in the play. Deciding *what* you want will, obviously, dictate how you go about *getting* what you want and help make clear what is *in the way* of getting what you want.

Step #5: What Is My Obstacle?
What is in the way of getting what I want? How do I overcome it?

An obstacle is the thing that prevents you from achieving your stated objective. If we could achieve our stated objective quickly and easily, there would be no dramatic conflict and hence, no play! Obstacles can come from the character's own inner workings; there may be something in his experience, internal makeup, or perceptions that blocks him and prevents him from achieving his goal, or the obstacle could be from an external source. The external source can be one or more people, or the character's environment or current circumstances.

Step #6: What Do I Do to Get What I Want?

How can I achieve my objective? What's my behavior? What are my actions? What is the character doing to get what she wants?

Uta Hagen was all about *doing*. She was interested in action. While the character uses her senses to connect with her environment and circumstances, the emphasis on the *senses* should not be mixed up with an emphasis on the character's *feelings*. It is not how the character feels that is important in creating dramatic action, but rather what the character is doing (Hagen 1991).

THE TEN EXERCISES

Now that we've covered the six steps to approaching a script and character, let's look at the exercises Hagen developed to address specific problems that the actor might encounter while developing a role and a character. Each exercise is created in such a way that the actor can work on the exercise alone.

Exercise #1: Physical Destination

This exercise is designed to help the actor understand what causes her character to move from one place to another.

Physical life on stage must be motivated. Such motivation can happen consciously or subconsciously. Psychology and surroundings dictate movement on stage from place to place. In this exercise the actor explores two or three minutes of behavior as she tries to accomplish a simple task. The exercise needs to have a beginning, a middle, and an end. The actor should note her destinations; that is, where she is compelled to go. Every step of that journey is motivated both conscious and unconscious thoughts and should be carefully noted by the actor. Understanding what motivates behavior will help the actor to always justify any movement on stage and make that movement truthful.

Exercise #2: Fourth Side

This exercise is designed to help the actor to embrace the **fourth side** or

fourth wall, as it is more commonly called. The fourth wall is the invisible wall that separates the audience from the playing space on stage.

In this exercise, the actor either places or receives an imagined telephone call. The actor must carefully determine his given circumstances, his goal (what he wants from the imaginary person on the other end of the phone), and his obstacle to achieving that goal. The aim is to engage in a realistic and truthful phone conversation that the audience can clearly observe while the actor remains unself-consciously engaged in the task of speaking on the phone; making his focus the engagement with the imaginary character on the other end of the phone rather than the awareness of the audience. This exercise helps the actor to create a realistic space and fully invest in the physical world that he has created.

Exercise #3: Changes of Self

We all have multiple aspects to our personalities. This exercise is designed to help the actor to understand the many different aspects of her own behavior.

This exercise, much like exercise #2, involves speaking on the phone. This time, however, the actor will speak to three imaginary people on the phone. Based on the actor's different relationships with these three individuals, the nature of the phone call and the actor's use of self while she is on the phone will be drastically different. The actor will undoubtedly notice great changes in vocal use, her own physical life, and her use of idiomatic expressions while speaking to these three very different people. If Hagen believes that the material needed to play all characters exists within the actor, this exercise is designed to show the actor how many different kinds of characters are already living within her.

Exercise #4: Moment-to-Moment

How do you repeat a given action night after night after night in a play and make it appear as if it is the first time that you are doing it? The first time you find an action, it is truthful. Repetition of the same action can quickly lose truth. The common actor's expression designed to inspire freshness and truthfulness on stage is "Give it the illusion of the first time." (An actor I knew years ago was in one of the longest-running shows in Boston, *Shear Madness*. He and his cast mates had this joke instead: "Give it the illusion of the five-hundredth time.") This exercise is designed to help actors to make repeated moments on stage fresh and interesting.

In this exercise, the actor imagines an urgent need to find an object that he has misplaced. He must create detailed given circumstances, an objective, and very high stakes if he fails to accomplish the objective. He must envision an environment that is believable; that is, if he is urgently searching for keys or a cell phone, he must replicate on stage an environment in which these items could be believably lost (such as a very disorganized book bag, or a messy room with laundry everywhere). When we truly look for a lost item in life, the frantic hunt for the item has distinct movements and moment-to-moment action.

This exercise will test the actor's ability to believe in and to make real each individual moment on stage in such a way that he can, time and again, execute the action with believability, precision, and truth.

Exercise #5: Re-creating Physical Sensations

This exercise helps the actor to endow an object on stage with qualities that it does not in fact possess.

This is an important skill in the theatre. For example, if you have ever seen a sword fight on stage, actors treat the stage swords as though they are deadly weapons, when in fact they are made dull to help keep the actors safe. An actor drinking scotch on stage is drinking water or another nonalcoholic substance. Actors having a hot cup of tea in a scene may be having lukewarm apple juice. An actor swallowing a bottle of pills on stage just had ten Tic Tacs.

In this exercise, the actor must endow selected objects with imaginary qualities.

The actor will choose five objects. She must identify all the ways that each selected object—with its imagined qualities—could affect her. She will interact with each item, imagining and enacting very specifically the sensory effect associated with the object, and will repeat the interaction again and again until she can be certain of being able to replicate it truthfully and honestly each time she must do so on stage.

Exercise #6: Bringing the Outdoors on Stage

This is another exercise to help the actor to believably create environment on stage. Where are we more alive and aware of our surroundings as human beings than in nature? Many plays take place in nature or have scenes that take place in an outdoor environment. The actor needs to create the sense of an outdoor environment for the audience.

In this exercise, the actor must decide upon a very specific environment, be it a beach (as the actor chooses to use in *Uta Hagen's Acting Class*), a porch, or a field under a starry sky. The actor decides what objects exist in this environment and must specifically envision how he deals with the objects (does hot sand burn his feet? does an ant crawl in his swim trunks?). The actor must inhabit this outdoor world truthfully, making an audience see the environment of his imagination specifically.

Exercise #7: Finding Occupation While Waiting

Hagen maintained that human beings are never just standing there doing nothing; people are always in action. In this exercise, the actor examines the behaviors that people engage in while they are waiting.

The actor must imagine that she is waiting for something or someone. She must have a strong sense of where she is going and where she has just come from. She also must have a very clear understanding of the specific environment that she is waiting in. She must explore how her imagined given circumstances and moment before affect her behavior while she waiting. What does she do in this environment under this set of circumstances? Her behavior will be very different if she has just had a marriage proposal, is late for work and fears being fired, or is waiting while she desperately needs to use the bathroom. The actor must note her specific behavior moment-to-moment under the set of circumstances she has envisioned.

Exercise #8: Talking to Yourself

It is one of the most feared and dreaded things the actor will encounter. It is scarier than a shark and a python in a dark alley at midnight. It is the soliloquy.

Talking to yourself on stage is weird. There is no other character to bounce anything off of. To the actor it can often feel untruthful and unnatural. This exercise is designed to make talking to yourself on stage less weird by investigating how you talk to yourself in regular life.

Hagen says that we talk to ourselves aloud in order to solve problems or gain control over a situation that feels out of control. The first time I found myself driving up and down the ridiculously steep hills of San Francisco, I was terrified. I swore colorfully. I told myself, aloud, that I was an excellent driver (à la the movie *Rain Man*). This was all fitting research for this exercise. Noticing how and when we talk to ourselves aloud is the first step to making such behavior truthful and honest on stage.

In this exercise, the actor must envision a circumstance that would compel him to speak to himself aloud. The actor must specifically create his given circumstances and environment and determine what is at stake. The actor must experience how he would truthfully talk to himself under this set of circumstances.

Once the actor understands this, any soliloquy, be it contemporary or classical, will have a greater degree of authenticity.

Exercise #9: Talking to the Audience

Direct address. Shakespeare used it all the time. Ferris Bueller does it in *Ferris Bueller's Day Off*. In early *Sex and the City* episodes, Carrie Bradshaw does it. Direct address is when the character breaks the fourth wall and speaks directly to the audience.

How do we make direct address truthful? In this exercise, the actor chooses a story or event that she desperately needs to share. She envisions a specific person sitting in the audience with whom she needs to share it. She must decide her given circumstances, objective, and obstacle.

After she becomes comfortable telling her story to this specific imagined person in the audience, she then retells the story, expanding it to include three or four imagined people. By making the target of her story very specific, she will make the direct address truthful, targeted, and effective.

Exercise #10: Historical Imagination

This exercise combines the lessons learned in the previous nine exercises.

The actor chooses a character from a play, which must be set in a different time period. He then follows the six steps for investigating a scene, choosing a specific task for this character to execute. The character may be ironing a shirt or writing a letter. It would be helpful to choose a task that this character is likely to perform in the play. Because the actor must make the place very specific, endow objects with distinct qualities, and understand his specific motivations for movement from moment to moment, he will likely need the entire skill set previously investigated through the other exercises.

Thus Hagen helps the actor to create the first bridge between the world of the studio and the world of the play. So often acting exercises can seem like just that: exercises. The challenge for the actor often becomes how to specifically apply the lessons learned to stagecraft. In this final exercise, Hagen shows the actor how these lessons can be directly applied to the world of the play (Bartow 2006).

What's It Like to Train Under This System?

THE CRITICS

If there are critics of Uta Hagen's books and exercises, they seem to be living in a hole underground somewhere. We have seen that many actor training methodologies and schools of thought are somewhat controversial. People have strong reactions favorably or unfavorably to many ways of training. But criticism of Hagen's work is very difficult to find. Perhaps it is because her work is so practical. The lessons and exercises can really be used to complement other forms of training and systems of preparation and rehearsal.

THE FANS

Uta Hagen's work is practical and intuitive. Her lessons are just that: lessons. What she has created is not a "system" or a formula, but an unpretentious group of tools that served her in her own work and that she, unselfishly, decided to share with the world. Hagen was articulate. She found ways of working that created a bridge between the sensory world and the world of action. She found a means for actors to access their inner selves without getting lost inside of themselves.

As an actor, Hagen knew how to make a performance fresh and new each night. Her lessons as a teacher seem to help many actors do just that.

WHERE TO GO FOR MORE INFORMATION

The best place to start is by reading Hagen's book *A Challenge for the Actor*. In tandem with this, I would recommend watching the wonderful DVD *Uta Hagen's Acting Class*, published by Applause books and currently available for purchase online.

Many teachers and programs weave Hagen's exercises and work into their other teachings. The most authentic and unadulterated training in pure Hagen technique is most likely available at HB Studios, where Hagen began her teaching. HB Studios now has the Hagen Institute (hbstudio.org/classes/the-hagen-institute), dedicated exclusively to her teachings.

10

Viewpoints

Theatre should resist certainty. —ANNE BOGART

It is difficult to explain Viewpoints. This is because the term refers to something that is entirely visceral. It is a means of creating theatre that relies on an instinctual, kinesthetic sense rather than on intellectual, cerebral sense. By its very nature it accesses an actor's instincts, getting the overly analytical brain to move to the back seat for a little bit while a wiser, intuitive self drives the bus.

What exactly is Viewpoints? Let's begin by explaining what it isn't. Viewpoints is not a training system in the same sense as the other training systems that we have looked at so far. What do I mean by this? It does not provide tools for analysis. It does not provide a set of steps for understanding a script. It does not provide a linear or methodical approach to attacking a scene. The best way to describe Viewpoints is that it is a kind of vocabulary. It is a way of explaining amorphous physical concepts like space and time and movement. It is a way of working, or, perhaps more specifically, a way of discovering theatre. It is best defined as a philosophy, a way of approaching theatre that always keeps the social and aesthetic value of theatre at the forefront. However you chose to define or explain Viewpoints, it is a concept that values the cohesiveness of the ensemble, and it is a way of thinking that is very much interested in investigating how actors tell stories through movement and composition.

Before I launch into more details about where Viewpoints came from, and before I try to explain more about what it is, I want to take you to Italy. That's right, Italy; for it is in Italy, and through a very specific experience in Italy, that Viewpoints work first fully made sense to me.

One day I was in a little Italian village, on a break from teaching acting at a summer program outside of Venice (see, sometimes being an acting teacher is a nice thing). It was a lovely town with cobblestone streets, and dim lamps, and drizzling rain, and charming shops that were selling dark purple bottles of wine and bright green olives from oaken barrels. It was the kind of magical place you'd want an Italian village to be, the kind of place that makes you forget that you have things back in America like cats that need flea medication and a phone bill that needs to be paid.

Walking through a narrow corridor, I came upon a sight that will always stay with me. A group of cats, about ten in total, appeared behind a wrought iron fence enclosing a crumbling stone building with several sets of steps and two small entryways. The cats had little awareness of me, the voyeur, and were all perfectly attuned to one another. They listened to each other with the kind of wise, visceral knowledge that only animals are in full command of. When one cat moved, another followed. When one jumped up on the steps, another jumped down. When one cat moved to the left, another moved to the right. The scene behind that wrought-iron fence was one of constant, harmonious balance. It revealed a space of perfect, fluid composition—a painting that was in perpetual motion. The cats operated as one entity; unified, balanced, and attuned. They were in perfect relationship with one another, maintaining a constant sense of tension and connectedness with the space and between themselves.

What do a group of Italian cats have to do with actors, with theatre, and with Viewpoints technique? Everything! These cats were the perfect creative ensemble. They listened to one another acutely. They took care of the aesthetic well-being of their space together. They functioned cooperatively to create an environment that was balanced and harmonious. They remained in a kind of constant physical dialogue both with each other and with the space. They intuitively understood when to move and how to move.

And this is when it occurred to me: human beings do not innately do this anymore. Once upon a time, when humankind roamed the African savannah, our focus was expansive, taking in all of the information that was around us. Our animal lives depended on this broad awareness. As we grew into a more advanced society, as the threat of being eaten by the saber-toothed tiger was gradually replaced by modern tasks and preoccupations, our focus became narrower and narrower. Now our circle of awareness is limited—sometimes to an interior experience that shuts out all the information around us. Space closes down, and closes us off from truly listening and reacting. Without a full awareness of space there can be no true awareness of time, as space and time walk hand in hand.

This moment in a small Italian village, watching cats on steps and eating cornmeal cookies out of the bottom of my purse, is the moment that it all became clear. This is what Viewpoints work was meant to teach us. It was meant to help actors to be as free and as in tune with space, with time, and with each other as that group of cats. I began to see that this tool, this way of seeing the world of theatre, can help the actor return to the level of animal awareness needed to truly inhabit stage space.

Viewpoints work is a method for helping actors to see and hear and experience and react. The cats, without written language, without cars to drive or shoes to buy or cell phones to answer or the other modern demands that close us down and lock us inside of ourselves, knew how to do this. Viewpoints work gives actors a tool to relearn how to be.

Where Did It All Begin?

MARY OVERLIE

It is fitting that a philosophy about theatre that emphasizes movement and composition grew out of the world of dance. In the 1970s, choreographer Mary Overlie, a performer and teacher working primarily with postmodern dance, developed the idea of the **six viewpoints**. Overlie describes the genesis of her work this way on her website, Six Viewpoints, a Deconstructive Approach to Theatre:

> The project of the Six Viewpoints was formulated in the landscape of Montana. In this environment distance has a physical impact on the body. The combination of high prairie and mountains inundates you with a sense of space and perspective. Man-made structures appear to be nothing more than arbitrary thoughts that change in the sweep of time. The voice of this land counsels you to learn to use perspective as a tool and to cut deeply into what concerns you. This is the point of view of the Viewpoints.
>
> In Montana the light seems to come from under your feet. Space becomes a primary language for the mind. Much work has been done on the Viewpoints site over the years but the voice of perspective has never been altered.
>
> I was given the concept that you can use your mind to move and change definitions but it is necessary to ground these thoughts in physical reality. I was taught to use the concepts of systems and logic, not as a set of rules, but to create a fluid dialogue. I learned to respect, rather than to fear deconstruction. This lesson is now articulated again and again in the Six Viewpoints process as a primary tool for creativity.
>
> These early influences allowed me to conceive of the idea that theater had a basic working language and that I could find it if I kept looking. Eventually I found the Six Viewpoints. The Viewpoints process reduces performance to a code. This code acts like a flexible measuring device, much like a transit and rod used in surveying for mapping land. The Viewpoints, like the transit and rod, were devised to reveal structure. The structure. The structure we see through the Viewpoints is made in six basic windows of perception that are used to create and view theater. (Overlie)

The Six Viewpoints

Overlie defined the six viewpoints as:

SPACE: The ability to perceive, see, and feel relationships physically

SHAPE: The ability of the actor/dancer to feel and to see physical form

TIME: The capability to perceive duration

EMOTION: An ability to understand and experience states of being

MOVEMENT: The ability to experience kinetic sensation

STORY: The capacity to understand a collected sequence of information and arrange it logically (Overlie)

ANNE BOGART AND TINA LANDAU

As we have seen already in this book, any good idea is born out of other good ideas. Perhaps even more importantly, we can see that a good idea, one that originates in the passion of its creator and her genuine hunger to understand something and to describe her understanding, creates a kind of revolution in creative thinking. Mary Overlie's ideas were born out of her own experience and her own questioning. She was also influenced by other great creative minds working at the same time who were trying to understand, not only what made dance "dance," but why dance was important. Overlie and other postmodern artists sought to understand and name dance's values and to describe how it fit into a larger artistic and social tapestry.

In 1979, theatre director Anne Bogart met Mary Overlie while both were on the faculty of NYU. Anne Bogart saw an immediate translation of Overlie's work in dance to theatre performance. Over the next ten years, Bogart worked with colleague and creative partner Tina Landau to expand Overlie's ideas into nine **physical viewpoints** (Bogart 1995).

In *The Viewpoints Book*, Bogart and Landau define the intertwined ideas of viewpoints and **composition**. They present Viewpoints as a philosophy turned technique for training theatre performers, a tool to build ensemble and to create stage moment. They identify it as a language to describe principles of movement through time and space; a kind of actor shorthand for articulating what happens on stage and in a stage space. They define composition as a process of identifying and weaving together different elements of this theatre grammar to create a realized and complete work for the stage (Bogart 1995).

In other words, Viewpoints is a tool that looks at specific elements of time and space, breaking those elements down so that they can be explored and expressed by the actor. It is both a way of training performers to think about how to use, understand, and operate in space and time in order to tell a story, and it is a means of exploring text and storytelling from various vantage points. Ultimately all of the components—that is, the individual viewpoints—combine together in various permutations and combinations to form composition.

PHYSICAL VIEWPOINTS

It is difficult to create composition without an awareness of the physical viewpoints. Bogart and Landau break the physical viewpoints into two categories: viewpoints of time and viewpoints of space.

Viewpoints of Time

TEMPO: The speed at which an action is performed. It can be performed quickly, slowly, or at any tempo in between.

DURATION: How long an action is allowed to continue for. Duration identifies a specific action's beginning, middle, and end point. It describes when one action needs to close and another action needs to commence.

KINESTHETIC RESPONSE: A spontaneous physical reaction to physical movement that occurs outside of one's self.

REPETITION: Repeating the movements, gesture, tempo, or shapes of others.

Viewpoints of Space

SPATIAL RELATIONSHIP: The distance between people in space.

TOPOGRAPHY: The physical landscape in which you are working; for instance, a grid (like a checkerboard). Topography describes a sense of vertical space (height) as well as horizontal space.

SHAPE: A body as it is appears in a space.

GESTURE: Gesture can be described in two categories:

- **literal**, behavioral gestures (that is, the gestures that we make in everyday life, such as scratching your head or rubbing your eyes)
- **expressive** gestures (that is, gestures that express abstract feelings or concepts, such as outspread arms to express the concept of eternity, a tucked-in head to express shame)

ARCHITECTURE: The tangible components of the space surrounding you (such as a doorway, a platform, or a window)

What Does It All Mean?

But what do these viewpoints *mean*? Once we have identified these elements of space and time, how can they be used by the performer?

As Tina Landau explains in the book *Viewpoints*,

> There are as many different ways to work on the Viewpoints in rehearsal as there are rehearsal approaches.... As training, the Viewpoints function much as scales do for a pianist or working at the barre does for the ballet dancer. It is a structure for practice, for keeping specific "muscles" in shape, alert, flexible. The actor, in the case of the Viewpoints, exercises awareness (awareness of the different Viewpoints), the ability to listen with the entire body, and a sense of spontaneity and extremity. The actor trains to take in and use everything that occurs around her, and not to exclude anything because she thinks she knows what is good or bad, useful or not. The Viewpoints enable performers to find possibility

larger than what they first imagine—whether it is in creating a shape they didn't know their body was capable of or in discovering a range of unexpected gestures for a character. By using the Viewpoints fully, we eliminate the actor's ability to state, "My character would never do that." By using the Viewpoints fully, we give up our own heady decisions and judgments. By using the Viewpoints fully, we give ourselves surprise, contradiction and unpredictability. . . .

The Viewpoints are practiced each day in rehearsal, at first separately and, after some time, together. Each rehearsal might begin with a twenty-minute Viewpoint session in which the actors will work together in an "improvisory" fashion. The only set structure is the notion of the Viewpoints. (Bogart, Landau 2005)

To try to understand what Landau means, let's look at two of the viewpoints that she mentioned above: the viewpoints of shape and gesture. Since Viewpoints is something clear to do but rather obtuse to describe, here is a page from my own journal from when I worked on Viewpoints with members of Anne Bogart's company.

Session 1: Shape
Begin to explore shape.
Stand alone in space. Focus on your body. Notice shape your body is making.

- Exaggerate this shape that you are naturally making.
- Drop this. Create shapes that are angular, linear. Use your whole body, especially parts you don't want to use.
- Add curves and circles. Let one shape evolve in space.

Shape Floor Exercise
Divide group into two lines. One at a time each individual moves through space from one side of the room to the other (much like floor work in dance class) in an angular fashion, mimicking an ancient Egyptian relief carving.

While moving across the floor, lead alternately with the head, center, tail, arms, and legs.

Repeat the floor exercise, this time finding softer, gentler lines. Soften the edges of the angular movements discovered. Move toward rounder shapes.

Repeat again, this time alternating sharp and soft movements. Have an interplay of angles and rounder shapes, paying attention to the hands as an extension of the core.

Repeat motion across the floor again, this time finding barely discernible, subtle shapes. What is the inner life such shapes express and communicate? Do they exist and express themselves randomly or in patterns? Are they repeatable?

Moving out of the lines to movement through the room. How might the shapes and gestural life you have discovered impact others, and how might you be impacted by their discoveries?

Session 2: Gesture

Begin to explore gesture.

Find object or person that interests you, and extend your hand toward the person with intention (what do you want from them?).

Perform this gesture slowly, then quickly. How does tempo change the quality of the action?

Remember this movement/gesture. Put it in your repertoire to repeat later.

Now find a behavioral gesture from everyday life (scratching, tucking a piece of hair behind your ear, smoothing your shirt). Repeat it. Let it evolve. Let it become stylized. Let it become realistic.

Now, we will work with expressive gesture, a gesture that is not literal but that describes the essence or quality of something such as infinity, freedom, horror, or rapture.

What is behind the movement? What is its inner life?

What is the beginning, middle, and end of the movement?

Session 3: Shape and Gesture
Define shape and gesture.

- Begin traveling through space with a specific shape. Allow that shape to be changed by the other shapes that you encounter.

- After several minutes, incorporate gesture. First, find an expressive gesture. Notice others' expressive gestures. What shape does it take? Work with the Shapes you see and your own expressive gesture.

- Next, investigate a literal gesture. Alternate freely between literal gesture, expressive gesture, and shape as you move through the space. Allow yourself to be changed by the shapes and gestures that you encounter as you move through the space.

The viewpoints may be explored by using the full space in a flowing manner, in a line (called lane-work), or by moving across an imaginary grid that the mind's eye lays out on the floor like a checkerboard. As you can see from the exercises above, initially each viewpoint is addressed in isolation. This allows the performer to fully explore the specific qualities of space and time that that viewpoint represents in that given moment. After individual viewpoints have been explored, they might be combined in a working session. As the viewpoints are combined, new discoveries emerge. Eventually, a very exciting thing happens. All nine viewpoints are combined in an improvisation called Open Viewpoints, where the actor explores the viewpoints in a spontaneous, improvisational composition based on the physical information that the room and fellow actors present. Sometimes Open Viewpoints sessions contain music. Later on in the process dialogue may be incorporated.

THE VOCAL VIEWPOINTS

In addition to the physical viewpoints, Bogart and Landau also define the vocal viewpoints. I think it is worth noting that, in my particular experience, while the physical viewpoints are widely known and practiced, the vocal viewpoints are less so. Perhaps the reason for this is that we already have a kind of vocabulary, through various practitioners of voice, for describing the elements of voice and sound, whereas, prior to Bogart's work, we had less of a vocabulary in actor training to describe space and time.

The aim of the vocal viewpoints is to investigate sound in much the same way that the physical viewpoints address movement. They acknowledge the fact that human sound has embedded psychological meanings and work to develop in the actor an awareness of pure sound that is entirely separate from linguistic meaning. Like any vocal exploration, these viewpoints also aim to expand the actor's vocal range, which may have become narrowed over time by habit and misuse. Through this process, the actor can develop a greater appreciation and understanding of sound and learn to use her vocal instrument in a fuller and more dynamic way.

The vocal viewpoints differ slightly from the physical viewpoints (Bogart 1995). You will recognize the first several:

- Tempo
- Duration
- Repetition
- Kinesthetic response
- Shape
- Gesture
- Architecture

Here they are related to sound rather than to space and time. In addition to these familiar viewpoints, we have the inclusion of

- Pitch
- Dynamic
- Acceleration/Deceleration
- Timbre
- Silence

The vocal viewpoints, like the physical viewpoints, are explored one at a time, first by the individual and later in an ensemble setting. Like the physical viewpoints, they are eventually combined and added to dialogue work. Once sound has been explored in and of itself, uncovering its inherent meaning and the strengths and limitations of the actor's instrument, it can be re-incorporated into sound that holds meaning (linguistic sound). Then, when sound is reunited with speech, the meaning cannot help but be richer and fuller.

WHY DO WE NEED THE VIEWPOINTS?

According to Bogart and Landau, the viewpoints offer a different and much-needed approach to creating theatre. Stanislavsky's system, they feel, has not changed or evolved over the years and is misunderstood in American training. They also believe that the system overemphasizes psychological motivation and does not appropriately factor in physical motivations.

The danger with relying on a psychologically based system rather than a way of working driven by physical impulse is that the actor often attempts either to generate a pre-programmed emotion or to replicate a moment of success in the theatre. Bogart and Landau believe that Viewpoints training allows the actor to have a spontaneous and truly organic human response to situations and to space. A heightened awareness of space and time can drive the actor to make choices out of an instinctive, almost biologically driven response to information, either increasing the reality of a psychological situation or eliminating the need for that drive entirely.

What's It Like to Train Under This System?
THE CRITICS

There are very few critics of Viewpoints that I am aware of. As a system of training and rehearsal one must keep in mind that it is relatively new and not necessarily in as widespread use as other methods that have been kicking around for a longer time. This may be part of the reason why there is little published criticism on this training. The few anecdotal criticisms that I have encountered are more in regard to the vocal viewpoints than the physical viewpoints (the concerns being the way breath is described and engaged in the vocal viewpoints). The beauty of being a kind of "alternate" training system is that, as with any countercultural movement, one almost has to seek it out; and, in general, if one is seeking it out, it is a fairly safe assumption that one is predisposed to respond favorably to it.

THE FANS

The fans of Viewpoints are many. Viewpoints melds acting disciplines with physical disciplines in a unique and unprecedented way. For adept physical actors with an acute kinesthetic sense, it can be a wonderful entry point. For actors who are challenged with their own sense of physical awareness, the physical viewpoints can serve to connect and open them in a way that movement disciplines may not be able to.

WHERE TO GO FOR MORE INFORMATION

I often feel that the real danger with Viewpoints training is that it may not be delivered to a new learner in its most pure and credible form. Having been fortunate enough to work directly with members of the SITI Company (Anne Bogart's theatre company), I have seen the training at its source. I have also, in my career, seen some bastardized attempts to interpret and replicate the training that I feel have fallen very short. Had I just experienced those bastardized versions, I might walk away scratching my head and saying, "What *is* this and what's all the fuss about?" For this reason it is important to get training as close to the source as possible.

The SITI Company (http://siti.org/content/training) currently offers fall and spring training and a variety of workshops and master classes, both in New York City and at their summer home in Saratoga Springs, New York.

You may also want to read *The Viewpoints Book*, by Anne Bogart and Tina Landau. This is almost a "how to" guide for ways to implement Viewpoints with a theatre company. *Viewpoints*, by Anne Bogart, offers more of an exploration of theatre and ways of thinking about theatre than a hands-on guide. The two books complement each other very well.

11

The Suzuki Method

If your productions are only talking to people with whom you share a common language and culture—that's entertainment. But if the work is appreciated by those outside your language, culture, and values—that's art. The theatre has a language barrier against multinational participation, so my goal is to diminish that language barrier.

—Tadashi Suzuki

Any conversation about Viewpoints training cannot help but flow into a conversation about the Suzuki Method. Anne Bogart's SITI Company intertwines the two training disciplines. While they are very distinct from one another, they are complementary systems of training; where you find one you quite often find the other.

The Suzuki Method of Actor Training, as it is called, was developed by Tadashi Suzuki. Don't confuse this Suzuki Method with another Suzuki Method, developed by Shin'ichi Suzuki, which is not a theatre training methodology at all, but a method for teaching music to young children. Sign up for *that* training and you won't learn too much about acting, but I bet you'll come out of it playing a mean violin.

Who Is Tadashi Suzuki?
Tadashi Suzuki is an acclaimed Japanese director, still working today, and

the founder of the Suzuki Company of Toga (SCOT) in Toga, Toyama, Japan.

Suzuki's main interest is in restoring the sense of the actor's whole body, allowing the actor to use the full range of the body's expressivity onstage. Like Viewpoints training, this system does not dwell in the territory of psychology. Rather, it is a physical discipline, drawing its inspiration from a wide range of art forms, including ballet, both traditional Japanese and traditional Greek theater, and martial arts.

A Synthesis of Eastern and Western Traditions

Tadashi Suzuki had always been interested in traditional Japanese forms of theatre such as Noh and Kabuki. But it was not until he saw a production of Noh theatre in Paris, in 1972 that the art's true power hit him. Something about seeing the traditional Japanese form of theatre outside of Japan, where it had to transcend language and culture to communicate with an audience, stunned him. It was here where he fully realized the how truly profound theatrical tradition could be. He spent the next years exploring ways to weave together traditional Japanese theatrical forms with Western forms. Suzuki formulated his actor training system, now known as the Suzuki Method. His experimentations generated a new kind of theatre that was physically based and visually stunning (Goto 1989).

Basic Principles

Suzuki explains that the main goal of his training method is to bring forth the actor's innate ability for physical expression. His interest is in those movements and physical ways of being that have universality, carrying meaning across different cultures. Much like Anne Bogart, Suzuki seeks to create a kind of physical grammar that, once assimilated into the actor's body, can be used to articulately create and realize theatre. When one is first learning a foreign language, one concentrates on the way that language is technically constructed. Eventually, as one gains proficiency, grammar becomes second nature. Sentences, paragraphs, and conversations can be created without a conscious awareness of the component technical parts. Unlike Viewpoints, which seeks to name and create a grammar so that elements of space and time can be articulated, Suzuki training seems interested in creating a grammar so that such elements, rather than being articulated, can be assimilated into the body to a point where the body is no longer conscious of the grammatical elements.

Suzuki's training emphasizes

- A kind of physical crispness, precision, and profound energizing of both the body and the voice; a belief that an energized body "speaks" even in stillness
- The importance of concentration
- A connection to the ground

THE GROUND

Suzuki believes that actors must develop an intuitive understanding of their connection to the ground, which aids them in developing an awareness of the body's core. It is the body's core that initiates and expresses movement. Suzuki holds that it is only through this strong ground connection that the body's core can be freed, allowing the actor to move fully. Suzuki training seeks to develop within the actor the capability to work with ease and fluidity even in the most challenging of physical circumstances.

THE OPPOSITION OF MOTION AND STILLNESS, OR, IN ANOTHER WORD . . . STOMPING!

I have an important word for you: stomping. Suzuki training involves an energized, specific, repeated striking of the floor. This places the actor's emphasis on the lower part of the body, which provides the connection to the ground. The lower portion of the body is strenuously engaged while the upper portion of the body remains relaxed and fluid. If we think about it, we tend to move the opposite way in modern American society: our customary awareness seems to be placed on the upper body, and the lower portion of the body just goes along for the ride.

With this movement we have not only a reversal, but a dichotomy; the lower portion of the body is in an energized motion while the upper portion of the body is in a kind of stillness. Here we have one of Suzuki's core ideas at play: the opposition of motion and stillness. The interplay of motion and stillness is something that fascinates Suzuki and is at the very center of his work. We can think of motion and stillness in his mind as a kind of yin and yang idea. In order to understand motion, we need to understand stillness. In order to understand stillness, we need to understand motion. The two opposing states are necessary, each needed for the other state to be perceived and understood.

We are so unaccustomed to this mode of movement in our society. Expect your first foray into Suzuki training to leave you sore. My first encounter with this training left me beyond wobbly. In traversing the floor with the level of energy and precision required by Suzuki training, my legs (one of the more muscular portions of my pretty un-muscular body) turned to Jell-O. I was walking rather suspiciously for days afterward. To watch someone who trains regularly with the system is both awe-inspiring and humbling, as the training requires true mental and physical discipline and concentration. It is not for the faint of heart or the faint of calves.

Although the training is physically based, the technique offers far more than this.

Actor and teacher Paul Budraitis explains:

> Although the physical results of the training are significant and tend to be what is emphasized when describing the technique, it is actually the psychological side of the training that is its more important part. This misconceived emphasis on the physical is understandable, of course. When you watch the training in process, what you see is a group of people intensely stomping the floor or very slowly moving across a room. What you don't see are the boundless worlds of imagination that

are providing context and intention for these movements. Ultimately, that is what the training seeks to develop: a connection to the body and the earth that allows the mind to be free to conjure and concentrate. My teacher Vesta Grabštait☐, who studied with Suzuki for five years at his training center in Togo, Japan, constantly emphasized this. She would say, and I would eventually experience, that no matter what the body is being asked to do, if an actor has a strong intention fueled by his or her imagination, that things as inconsequential as pain or discomfort "recede to the fiftieth plane," and what remains is an artist connected to the present moment with the entirety of their self. (Budraitis 2012)

THE BREATH AND LANGUAGE

At the very core of Suzuki's physical grammar is the actor's breath. Suzuki work teaches a kind of breathing that leads to release and focus. By focusing the breath in this way, the actor taps into something base and primal, an animal-like energy. Such a release of energy is at the core of human experience. It is something visceral rather than intellectual.

While this visceral, nonintellectual experience is vital to his approach, Suzuki also believes that the quest for universal meaning must incorporate and honor language. In some productions, this has meant using multiple languages simultaneously. While in a sense Suzuki's work aims to transcend language as it communicates across cultures, this has never meant abandoning it (Horowitz 2014).

THE SELF

Looking closely at Suzuki's work, not only in comparison to the other methodologies I have laid out in this book, but also in comparison to other practitioners of his time, his work strikes me as uniquely different. Suzuki's approach is unlike other theatre approaches in this way: he is not interested in the psychology of character, but in the psychology of self. He is not interested in the story of the playwright; he is interested in our universal human story.

Suzuki has argued that the modern world has dismembered our physical faculties and our essential selves. Suggesting that we all wish to reunite these parts of ourselves and to overcome our limitations, he believes that what becomes interesting for actors to explore and for audiences to watch is the way actors can overcome obstacles. For Suzuki, acting should be judged by the reasons the actor has to stand on a stage and he suggests that an actor's lack of skill often only displays an actor's physical limitations and personal oppressions. Valuing personal examination more than textual examination, he asks actors and audiences to consider whether or not the actor is only focused on speaking the words of a playwright or if the actor is able to transcend their limitations. (The Academy Literature and Drama Website)

What's It Like to Train Under This System?
THE CRITICS

It is easy to misunderstand the intention of Suzuki's work. I believe that to launch into the work without first understanding the theories and philosophies that drive it may lead the actor to a place of confusion. When misapplied and misunderstood, Suzuki work can produce an actor who works with too much force, whose only dynamics are *forte* and *mezzo forte*, and who works with stiffness rather than fluidity. In the worst case, without proper instruction, the highly athletic use of voice can lead to vocal strain.

As with any training system, it is vital that its teachers impart the method precisely and authentically, particularly given the highly physical nature of the Suzuki Method. Well taught and explained, this training can open up the vocal and physical instrument and the actor's spiritual and imaginative self with tremendous results. Poorly explained and incompletely taught, it can do quite the opposite.

THE FANS

I asked a former student of mine, Ronald Reeder, who received his Suzuki training at Louisiana State University, why he was a fan. His answer may interest you.

> There was a particular day we were doing scene work on Richard III. . . . I'm not sure what it was, but that was the day I felt like I finally understood what it was about.
>
> I was extraordinarily focused on my scene partner—actually my awareness of my surroundings in general was just about as heightened as I can ever remember. I felt super-engaged in the moment, like I had transcended myself and moved into some reality more important than the one I usually inhabit . . . And I realized that, from the first time I had done any Suzuki work, months before, this heightened focus, this ability to engage deeply, had always been the necessary result of these exercises—all I needed to do was recognize that it was there and embrace it. So it clicked for me that day.
>
> Then I had a revelation. All these great acting theorists and instructors, Stanislavski, Adler, Strasberg, Meisner, they all had very useful and important insights, but, in the end, they were simply alchemists, fumbling in the dark, searching for the right spells and incantations. Tadashi Suzuki, in stark contrast, is a scientist in the modern sense . . . the work is concrete and replicable, with clear and demonstrable results, just as all science is.
>
> Now, don't get me wrong. I haven't made Suzuki the center of what I'm about as an actor—indeed, where I'm at right now as an actor essentially reflects where most university actor training programs are; that is, I use some of this and some of that, depending on the circumstances. But I do recognize Suzuki's work as being as important and groundbreaking as anything that preceded him. Indeed, his name ought to always be mentioned in the same breath as all those alchemists, maybe with an asterisk by his name to denote that he's the one using science, instead of magic.

WHERE TO GO FOR MORE INFORMATION

The SITI Company offers substantive Suzuki training in conjunction with Viewpoints training. The University of Washington Professional Actor Training Program also has Suzuki at the core of its training.

Two valuable books worth checking out are *The Art of Stillness: The Theater Practice of Tadashi Suzuki,* by Paul Allain, and *The Way of Acting: The Theatre Writings of Tadashi Suzuki*, by Tadashi Suzuki (translated by J. Thomas Rimer).

Spolin and Improv

Through spontaneity we are re-formed into ourselves. It creates an explosion that for the moment frees us from handed-down frames of reference, memory choked with old facts and information and undigested theories and techniques of other people's findings. Spontaneity is the moment of personal freedom when we are faced with reality, and see it, explore it, and act accordingly. In this reality the bits and pieces of ourselves function as an organic whole. It is the time of discovery, of experiencing, of creative expression.

—VIOLA SPOLIN

Often called the mother of improvisation for the theatre, Viola Spolin was a very important thinker in the American theater in the twentieth century. An accomplished director, she developed directorial and actor training techniques aimed at helping actors find choices through improvisational exercises that would enable them to live and to fully focus moment-to-moment onstage.

In the early 1930s, Spolin served as the drama supervisor for the Chicago Works Progress Administration's (WPA) Recreational Project. While working for the WPA, Spolin saw the need to develop a kind of theatre training that would help to bridge the cultural and ethnic barriers within the WPA's community. She began to develop games for her students in order to communicate complex ideas to them in a simple and direct way.

They say that necessity is the mother of invention, and the mother of improvisation would have probably agreed. This is a very different way for a theatre technique to have evolved. While Uta Hagen and Stella Adler developed their acting techniques from their own performance careers as actors—while the other methods of acting that we have looked at so far arose from a desire to create either a working process for actors or a way to revolutionize the theatre—Spolin's technique arose simply out of a necessity to communicate in a difficult set of circumstances. Once in an interview, Spolin explained, "The games emerged out of necessity . . . I didn't sit at home and dream them up. When I had a problem [directing], I made up a game. When another problem came up, I just made up a new game'" (Robinson, Roberts, and Barranger 1989). Spolin invented a whole new way of working based on a need in the moment.

Spolin went on to found the Young Actors Company in Hollywood. Later, she conducted workshops in her games with the Compass, the first professional, improvisational acting company in America. Her later work with son Paul Sills formed the foundation of the Second City Company in Chicago, an improvisational troupe still working today (Robinson, Roberts, and Barranger 1989). In 1963, Spolin published her games and exercises in a volume called *Improvisation for the Theater*. This text has become something of an improvisational bible for theatre students and teachers. A second volume of her work, *Theater Games for Rehearsal: A Director's Handbook*, was released in the mid-1980s.

The success of the Second City Company helped Spolin put a new kind of theatre on the map. At Second City, Improvisational Theatre, or "improv" (its shorthand name), was born. If you watch shows like *Whose Line Is It Anyway* or enjoy any kind of local improv troupe in your community, you can thank Viola Spolin and her son, Paul Sills. Improv is such a part of our theatre consciousness that it is hard to imagine a world without it.

Basic Principles

Spolin's improvisational work became known as Theatre Games. She could have termed her work "exercises" just as easily, but with "games" she chose to emphasize the idea of exploration through play. Sadly, we often lose sight of this idea as we're working in the theatre. Theatre is playful. By calling her work "games," Spolin automatically gave actors permission to explore and have fun.

Theatre Games are simple. As a training method, Spolin's games provide a way to make complex ideas about theatre simple and easily accessible. Every game that Spolin developed has a singular and specific focus. Each game is intended to get actors to stop thinking and to start doing, connecting them with their own creativity and their authentic, "real" selves.

The games take many forms. Some are designed to free the actor of tension. Some are designed to clear from the actor's mind the idea that words have specific and limited meanings. Other are designed to improve concentration. The range of games is expansive and highly variable. In short, for any acting challenge, Spolin has created a game to help actors explore it (Robinson, Roberts, and Barranger 1989). A single game addresses a single aspect of craft.

Playing one of Spolin's games allows the actor to operate in the moment. If an actor has to focus his attention fully on keeping a tennis ball in the air, there is no way that he can remain "in his head," focused on an intellectual concept or idea. By focusing on a single task within the structure of the game, the actor sidesteps pre-programmed choices and self-judgment, and inspiration and spontaneity are free to bubble forth. Spolin referred to this as **direct experience**, which she defined as "the premise that the intuitive must be accessed to incorporate intelligence, integrates mind and body, and produces spontaneous action and discovery in the act of doing" (Schwartz 2012a). We can see that Spolin's philosophy does not stress an intellectual approach, and instead aims for experiencing something in the moment through play that opens up the actor's intuitive and holistic senses. Through a state of playfulness, the mind and body unite, becoming fully involved in solving the problem at hand. This dedication to solving a specific task opens the actor to his own instincts, making him fully present and alive in the moment and opening up a world of skills that may be called upon in the service of any play.

AN EXAMPLE

As is the case with any training system that involves real-time experience more than an analytical, intellectual skill set, it is difficult to get the idea of Spolin's work by talking about it. To give you an idea of what it might be like to participate in one of her exercises, her student Gary Schwartz offers this description of an exercise. The game is called "Swat Tag."

> The game involves a group of people sitting in chairs, a "home base" (a chair or stool set out in front of the group), where the swatter (a rolled-up newspaper) is placed. The person who is "it" takes the swatter and moves into the audience and tags someone with the swatter. That person must then jump up and chase the swatter back to home base where the swatter has to put down the rolled news-paper on the home base and try to run back to where the tagged person was sitting and sit down in their chair before the other person can pick up the swatter and tag them back. If the runner makes it back to the chair without being tagged, the tagged person is now "it" and must tag someone else in the audience and take their chair in the same manner. If the original tagger is swatted before getting back to the seat, they both run back to home base and try again.

This sounds a lot like something you might do at summer camp that has nothing to do with theatre. Why is it a theatre training exercise? Read on . . .

> This game was a blast! Everyone was involved in it: the runners, and the rest of the audience, too. Afterwards, Viola asked us what happened to us. What happened physically and psychologically? The answers came back. "We had fun!" "We laughed!" "Our hearts raced and we were in a high state of alert."

"So your body had a physical reaction to it," Viola asked. "Yes, what else? What were you thinking about?"

"Nothing. Just the game." (Schwartz 2012b)

Being present in the moment—being *fully* present—is one of the actor's hardest tasks. A simple game such as this one not only demands all of the actor's attention and focus, but forces her to invest in the moment without knowing the outcome of the action. This game, like all of Spolin's games, is a simple task that teaches some of the greatest theatre lessons.

A WORD ABOUT SPOLIN AND SIDECOACHING

If you pick up one of Spolin's books, you will see a curious word next to each exercise. The word is **sidecoach**. The sidecoach functions as a kind of director, directing the exercise for the actor/players. He is the guide through the exercise who helps the players to play the game fully. An effective side-coach knows the rules of the game, giving the players helpful reminders and helping the actors to remain focused on the task at hand. Like any good athletic coach, an effective Spolin sidecoach makes the players feel supported and encouraged, never judged or restricted.

Spolin's Games Outside of the Theatre

Spolin's Theatre Games and improvisational techniques apply to much more than theater training. More importantly, because Spolin's games are so effective at teaching people to be fully committed to the moment and engaged as part of an ensemble or team, they are used in disciplines besides theatre:

> Spolin's games have developed currency beyond actor training, that is, in encountering techniques, self-awareness programs, and nonverbal communication studies. Viola Spolin's systems are in use throughout the country not only in university, community, and professional theater training programs, but also in countless curricula concerned with

educational interests not related specifically to theater. . . .

She has introduced her work to students and professionals in theater, elementary and secondary education, schools with gifted and talented programs, curriculum studies in English, religion, mental health, psychology, and in centers for the rehabilitation of delinquent children. She notes that "Theater Games are a process applicable to any field, discipline, or subject matter which creates a place where full participation, communication, transformation can take place." (Robinson, Roberts, and Barranger 1989)

Perhaps the greatest appeal of Spolin's improvisation training is a product of its original design; these tools were created to bridge cultural, linguistic, and socioeconomic gaps with the students that she was working with. The tools remain, today, a way of bringing together people with different life experiences in a team environment, focused on a singular task. As Gary Schwartz writes,

That was how Spolin conceived of improvisation. . . . It creates strong, unified teams made up of dynamic individuals all working to achieve for the sake of staying present and excited and fully involved in any endeavor. . . . Spolin's work operates from a different paradigm: non-authoritarian, non-intellectual, non-judgmental group agreement. Where one is a part of a whole; a fellow player in relation to others to your fullest capacity with the purpose of stepping into the unknown and exploring the possibilities. (Schwartz 2012a)

What's It Like to Train Under This System?
THE CRITICS

Spolin's Theatre Games teach life skills that can serve as a kind of metaphor for the theatre. If, through a game, the actor can fully commit to the present moment without supposition or projection of an outcome, she can transfer this lesson learned in the game to a lesson for the stage. If the actor can work together with her fellow teammates in the game to achieve an outcome, she can apply this connectedness to her work in an ensemble on stage.

For some actors, the connection between the game and the stage is too metaphorical. Those who do not respond well to the work find it hard to apply its lessons to real-world stage experience. "Spolin is for class. I've never seen a practical approach applied to a real-world situation unless the show is of a bizarre, improv nature," says my colleague, veteran actor Wayne LeGette. The translation from classroom experience to pragmatic and useful tools for stage situations feels like too broad a leap for some.

THE FANS

Spolin's improvisational games have woven their way, in some form, into many theatre training programs. In them are hints of improvisational work from Stanislavky and from Meisner's teachings, reinforcing the notion that all useful ways of approaching theatre borrow from one another and weave together in some way. Fans of Spolin believe that the games amp up self-awareness, creativity, and positive ensemble dynamics. The improvs teach an ability to problem-solve in the moment in a way that flexes creative muscles and strengthens the actor's imagination. Fans will argue that every actor worth his salt needs to understand and be comfortable to some degree in the world of improvisation. Spolin, having originated the idea of improv itself, is certainly the teacher most equipped for this job.

WHERE TO GO FOR MORE INFORMATION

Reading *Improvisation for the Theater*, Spolin's first book, is a great place to start. The Sills/Spolin Theater Works site is a center dedicated to preserving the work of Viola Spolin and Paul Sills. Their website, www.sillsspolintheaterworks.com/workshops, is a great resource for interested actors and lists upcoming workshops.

Grotowski

Theatre can exist without makeup, without autonomic costume and scenography, without a separate performance area (stage), without lighting and sound effects, etc. It cannot exist without the actor-spectator relationship of perceptual, direct, "live" communion. This is an ancient theoretical truth, of course, but when rigorously tested in practice it undermines most of our usual ideas about theatre.

—JERZY GROTOWSKI

Where Did It All Begin?

Grotowski asked the biggest question of them all: What is theatre? As he searched for the answer, other questions arose: What did it take for a production to exist? What was central to the art form and what was superfluous? What was the nature of the relationship between actor and spectator? Jerzy Grotowski's work revolutionized theatre and the way we think of theatre. He invited the world to see theatre as a spiritual union between actor and spectator, and theatres as sacred space.

Grotowski was a Stanislavsky-trained actor. Though Polish-born, he attended school in Moscow. His talent as a theatre director quickly became evident, and his directorial debut was the absurdist farce *The Chairs* by Eugène Ionesco in 1957 at the Stary Teatr (Old Theatre) in Krakow. After the premiere of *The Chairs*, the Laboratory Theatre gained increasing international interest.

We have seen over and over again that innovative thinkers and practitioners of the theatre start from a place of disharmony with the current state of the art. The fuel for innovation is dissatisfaction. Jerzy Grotowski was no different. Unhappy with the limitations of theatrical realism, in 1959 he created the Laboratory Theatre, gathering a small group of actors in Poland. There he began an investigation of theatre that would once again shake up the status quo.

Grotowski was invited to work in the United States and left Poland in 1982. It is here that we see another repeating theme: the assimilation of a great theatre thinker's ideas in America and a subsequent misunderstanding and misrepresentation of his training system. As Grotowski's innovative ideas gained steam in the United States, he grew more and more uncomfortable with the way that they were being understood and implemented. He quickly became so ill at ease with the interpretation of his work in America that, at the very peak of his success, he packed up and moved to Italy, establishing the Grotowski Workcenter in 1985. It was in Italy where Grotowski would spend the rest of his life and career, directing and experimenting, only now rather outside of the limelight of the international community (The Academy Literature and Drama Website).

TOWARDS A POOR THEATRE

In 1968, Grotowski published the groundbreaking book *Towards a Poor Theatre*. The book serves as a record of Grotowski's experiments with the Laboratory Theatre. More than that, it was a probing inquiry into the nature of theatre itself.

Grotowski sought to do two things in his investigation into the essential nature of theatre as he documented his thoughts and experiments in this book:

- To identify and define what made theatre a unique art form
- To understand the powerful relationship between actor and audience and how it could be used to affect social and political change

He wrote:

> I am a bit impatient when asked, "What is the origin of your
> experimental theatre productions?" The assumption seems to be that
> "experimental" work is tangential (toying with some "new" technique
> each time) and tributary. The result is supposed to be a contribution
> to modern staging—scenography using current sculptural or electronic
> ideas, contemporary music, actors independently projecting clownish
> or cabaret stereotypes. I know that scene: I used to be part of it. Our
> Theatre Laboratory productions are going in another direction. In the
> first place, we are trying to avoid eclecticism, trying to resist thinking of
> theatre as a composite of disciplines. We are seeking to define what is
> distinctively theatre, what separates this activity from other categories
> of performance and spectacle. Secondly, our productions are detailed
> investigations of the actor-audience relationship. That is, we consider
> the personal and scenic technique of the actor as the core of theatre
> art. (Grotowski 1968)

Grotowski knew this: theatre could never compete with cinema when it
came to creating spectacle. Cinema could provide the audience with special effects that simply couldn't be produced in live theatre. But theatre, he
maintained, could offer something that film could not: a relationship. The
relationship between live actor and live audience was something rare and
unique. With this in mind, Grotowski sought to identify the nature of the
relationship between actor and spectator. His aim was to bring a kind of
theatre to an audience that was "confronting, challenging and experiential.
It was a theatre not based so much on image (as in cinema or television) but
on the presence of the actor" (Jason Bennett Actor's Workshop).

WHAT IS POOR THEATRE EXACTLY?
Grotowski said, "If the stage cannot be richer than the text, then let it be
poorer" (1968).

Confronted with the superior technology of film to create visual richness, Grotowski decided to take theatre in the opposite direction. He advocated a kind of theatre that would strip away all unnecessary elements of production, leaving only the actor, spectator, space, and text. This was the idea of the **poor theatre**. Poor theatre was a theatre in which the fundamental concern was the relationship between the actor and the audience; it was not concerned with spectacle. Lights, costumes, and sound effects were all deemed unimportant. This was a huge departure from the European theatre of the nineteenth century, which prized elaborate costumes and sets. For Grotowski it was the actor's instrument—the "special effects" of the trained and nimble body and voice—that was at the core of theatrical power.

Stripping away the spectacle left only the actor on stage, raw and vulnerable, without anything to hide behind. This, Grotowski felt, was the true theatre: a theatre that was "poor," stripped down to its basics, as opposed to a "rich" theatre that was dressed to the nines, hiding its real substance behind flash.

THE HOLY ACTOR

Grotowski was interested in the spiritual communion that an actor and spectator enter into in a theatrical space. The idea of the theatre as a spiritual place is quite a lovely idea. I have often heard my more agnostically inclined students say that theatre is a kind of surrogate for religious experience for them. The theatre is a place where they feel not only a sense of true community, but a sense of spiritual belonging that they do not find elsewhere. It is a place where they come together to change and to be changed. Many of them have expressed this idea with, I'm quite certain, no working knowledge of Grotowski or his ideas.

To the idea of the poor theatre Grotowski added the idea of the **holy actor**. Grotowski saw theatre as having a kind of spiritual power that was capable of inspiring and eliciting change. Actors enter into a spiritual relationship with the space and with the spectator in the space. The line of thinking goes like this:

- When the actor enters a given performance space, the space
  is transformed into a kind of spiritual place, influencing
  the relationships of people inhabiting that space (much as a
  church, a temple, or another religious space affects the people
  in it).
- In this space a spiritual, "holy" relationship develops
  between actor and audience.
- In this place of communion, the actor can then challenge
  the audience. By viewing the actor in this spiritual space,
  the audience can be called upon to improve themselves and
  expand themselves.

In creating a kind of sacred experience and union, the theatre became more than entertainment; it became a pathway to understanding (Jason Bennett Actor's Workshop).

Poor theatre then was a means of exploring the most basic of theatrical elements in order to enhance communion between actors and audience, creating the holy actor. The play and the text was merely a vehicle for self and social exploration. Grotowski argued that "dramatic literature offered only a framework for actors' explorations of themselves" and that "only had meaning if it could enable actors and audiences to transcend stereotyped visions and conventional or habitual behavior's and responses" (1968).

THE GROTOWSKI-TRAINED ACTOR

Grotowski believed that the holy actor was an actor who was capable of using his body in heightened and unusual ways. By transcending customary physical limitations, the actor would "reveal his most true, most intimate self on stage. . . . The principle behind this was that the actor would set an example to the spectator, provoking them to see themselves as capable of change. By extension, this would inspire the spectator to think politically and to make changes in society" (Oxley 2006).

What does this mean? In short, this means that you, the actor training under Grotowski's psychophysical acting technique, will become a human pretzel.

It is here where I will take a painful jog down memory lane to recount my own experience training under the wonderful Grotowski practitioner Andrei Droznin. A more gentle soul than Andrei Droznin does not exist on earth. An intense yet smiling man, Polish-born like dear Grotowski himself, he is warm and welcoming, soft-spoken and kind. And yet . . . this man caused me more physical pain than anyone else on earth. Mind you, though petite and skinny, I am not a nimble physical creature. I recall a day when I was on a thick, blue mat trying desperately to do a split without literally splitting myself, and my body just wouldn't go down any further. Andrei Droznin came up behind me, and with one swift move of his firm hand on my shoulder—splat! I went into a split that had me walking like a farmer through a cow-pooped field for days. Droznin termed this level of physical discomfort "a special kind of pleasure." Yes, it was special, all right. And, I realized years and several tubes of tiger balm later, it was in the service of transcending my own physical limitations in order to inspire an audience.

I certainly was encouraged to go beyond my own physical limitations. In my case, the transformation was most unimpressive. I went from a physically stiff, inflexible creature to a slightly less stiff and inflexible creature. For many actors, however, the transformation, as Grotowski and Andrei Droznin intended, is absolutely astounding.

In 2002 I spent several months in Russia. Sitting in on a Grotowski class at the Schukin School at the Vakhtangov Institute in Moscow was an amazing experience. There are no words to truly describe what I saw there. Here was Grotowski's idea of the holy actor in play, where students seemed to do the physically impossible. They performed exercise after exercise on long mats, contorting their bodies into unrecognizable forms. This was stuff that would have made Cirque du Soleil performers blush. These actors truly rose above their own limitations—indeed most any human's physical limitations—and the result onstage was transformative. Actors trained in Russia in Grotowski move like circus performers. Their command over their physical bodies is unparalleled. Everything they experience as actors is expressed through the physical body. Bringing the body to its most heightened and nuanced way of functioning allows them to be fully expressive in their life onstage.

Elements of Grotowski Training

In addition to pushing the limits of customary physical boundaries, Grotowski-trained actors focus on these other elements:

Vocal training. To Grotowski, the human voice is like a musical instrument. During training actors may be called upon to sing or use heightened text (poetry).

Working in stillness. Much like Suzuki, Grotowski feels that the actor must be aware of and be able to use stillness in his work. Stillness leads to concentration. Concentration allows for inspiration.

Memory. Grotowski believed that the actor must draw on her own life experience in order to truthfully have communion with the audience.

What's It Like to Train Under This System?

THE CRITICS

Grotowski excavated theatre. He went into its very core to understand its inner workings like a philosopher or a scientist. His questions were not only about the craft of acting, but about the power of theatre and its place, role, and obligation in society. His thinking was revolutionary. In truth, Grotowski was such a complex thinker that his work can sometimes seem so obtuse or elusive. It is easy to misconstrue or misrepresent it. Without truly understanding the deep and beautiful philosophy that drove Grotowski's work, it would be easy to be puzzled by actor training under his system. My own experience was that of an incomplete understanding. As I was doing the painful exercises, I knew that they were designed to enable the actor to fully inhabit the body, but without fully comprehending Grotowski's philosophies at the time of my training, I received only a shadow of its meaning.

Perhaps more dangerous than an incomplete understanding of, in my case, very authentic and well-delivered training, is the greater danger of incomplete or not fully fleshed-out training. Grotowski training must be immersive and carried out over a long period of time to achieve the intended results. It requires very focused work with actors over a very long period of time. These conditions in modern training systems are not always possible. American programs often take a "smorgasbord" approach to training, especially to physical training disciplines, where many different physical systems may be sampled in a given training period. For Grotowski to have any staying power and any relevance for the actor, it needs to be delivered in a manner as close to the original practice as possible. An actor cannot simply take a Grotowski class or do a smattering of work in the discipline and expect any significant transformation For Grotowski to be effective, it needs an incredible amount of time, rigor, dedication and patience to blossom. So, with that in mind, you may want to reconsider signing up for the three-day Grotowski workshop I saw advertised on the internet. Paying for that three-day workshop might just make you into a Poor Pretzel. And that's not the kind of poor theatre that Grotowski was moving toward.

THE FANS

Grotowski's system is a way of thinking and being in the world. It enables the actor to develop his full physical, vocal, and spiritual potential. The authentically trained Grotowski actor is physically prepared for work in the theatre in a way that is drastically different from other training methodologies. Fully immersed Grotowski actors (and by that I mean actors who have studied this system of training for years, as I witnessed in the Russian Federation) are nearly superhuman in their physical command and aptitude. For the mere mortals who have authentic exposure to the training, but not the level of immersion that our Eastern European friends can access, the rewards can also be transformative. While such actors may not achieve the skill level of a circus performer, they definitely become more flexible, aware, physically engaged, strong, and malleable beings. When one sees a

Grotowski actor in action, one cannot help but be reminded that to be in the theatre is to be an artist of the highest caliber.

WHERE TO GO FOR MORE INFORMATION

Why not read *Towards a Poor Theatre*? Though dense at times, the ideas are fascinating and it is one of the most important books written about the theatre.

While an introductory training program may help you to get a taste of the nature of the training, for a truly transformative training experience, this actor thinks you need to head right to the source. The Eugene O'Neill Theater Center in Waterford, Connecticut, offers semester training programs at the Moscow Art Theatre. As part of this training program you will find an authentic experience training in Grotowski technique. For the serious, and I mean serious-serious, Grotowski experience, you can always learn Russian and pack up for the Schukin School at the Vakhtangov Institute in Moscow. I know two brave actors who did just that. And man, are they flexible . . .

14

Demystifying Vocal Training

We've talked a lot about actor training so far. Studying acting, strangely enough, is only one part of training yourself to be a professional actor.

If you are a trumpet player, your trumpet is your instrument. If you are a harpsichordist, your harpsichord is your instrument; but if you are an actor, your instrument is your voice and body. It is not enough to have great acting craft and technique. It is not enough to have a means of understanding and analyzing a script. If your voice and body cannot support the range of dynamic and vibrant choices that you make as an actor, your acting cannot live on stage. In the next two chapters, we will take a look at systems and methods for training the actor's voice and body.

Why Do Actors Need Voice Training?

A lot of people are confused initially about what voice training is. I began my teaching career, not as an acting teacher, but as a voice and speech trainer and coach. When I would tell people that I taught voice for actors they would say things like, "Oh, so you teach singing." It is the first assumption of the layperson, and it is a pretty logical one. Why do I say that it's a logical assumption? Singing is a heightened use of the human voice, and longevity as a singer requires good craft and proper technique. If a singer has not been trained to use her voice correctly, she can sound great for a few months or a few years or a few shows (depending on the demands that she is placing on her untrained instrument), but in time her voice will start to become hoarse. Singing will become more and more difficult. She may develop vocal nodes (nodules on the vocal folds caused by improper vocal use) that demand rehabilitation, medication, or even surgery. The singer, in short, needs to know what she is doing, because, when she is singing on stage, her voice is called upon to do very intense and athletic things on a repeated basis.

The speaking actor needs to learn to do exactly the same thing. The speaking actor also uses her voice in a highly athletic way. An untrained actor who does not know how to properly use her voice will, at some point, falter. She may be called upon in a play to scream, cry, cough, or whisper. If she does not know how to do this with proper technique, her voice, in all likelihood, will not last for the run of the play. She will likely develop hoarseness and vocal fatigue, and may even damage her voice.

But vocal safety is not the only reason to learn how to use the voice properly. The voice, along with the body, is the actor's means of human expression. In order to give transformative and truthful performances, the actor needs to cultivate an expressive, connected voice that is capable of a range of nuanced life. Quite simply, the actor's voice is the conduit through which the experience of the play is delivered to the audience.

We've talked about theatre being a heightened version of reality, and not a replication of reality itself. If you think about it, during our most heightened experiences in life—moments of extreme joy, terror, passion, or anguish—we are incredibly vocally and physically alive. Since we go to the theatre to see the most interesting, disturbing, touching, and affecting moments in life, it should follow that the actors touching us with these moments would be fully vocally and physically present and vibrant. The actor needs to train the voice in order to safely and capably meet these demands of the art form.

PRACTICAL THINGS THAT VOICE TRAINING HELPS THE ACTOR TO DO

Voice Training Helps the Actor to Stay Healthy

Studying the mechanics of the voice and breath will help the actor to properly use and support his vocal instrument. Voice training will also teach the actor all that his voice is capable of doing and increase his command of the voice in performance.

As we touched on above, sometimes the actor will be called upon, not only to speak on stage, but to make unusual and even risky demands on the voice. Voice training will help the actor learn how to perform what I call vocal extremes safely. This term refers to any extreme use of the voice, including

- Yelling or screaming on stage
- Keening (this happens a lot in Greek plays and some Irish plays—it's a kind of over-the-top mournful wailing
- Coughing (believe it or not, coughing can be really rough on the voice)
- Whispering (stage whispering is actually just as dangerous to the voice as screaming)
- Weird things you can't even think of right now! I once had to spend an hour coaching actors in a Shakespeare play on how to roar like a lion and bray like a donkey without hurting themselves (there are all kinds of ways to make a living, aren't there?)

Voice Training Helps the Actor to Be Clear and Articulate on Stage

Quite simply, voice training helps the actor to speak clearly and precisely so that everything that he says on stage can be easily understood by the audience. Theatre work is not the same as film work. On stage, our voices must move through a very large space, overcoming bad acoustics and any noises from inside or outside the building. We actors have to be prepared, and must do everything in our power, to speak clearly and resonantly so that our stories can be told and understood.

Voice Training Helps the Actor to Be Truthful on Stage

Voice training prepares the actor to give and receive energy on stage.

A pressed, strained voice is a sure sign the actor is attempting to manufacture intensity rather than responding truthfully to his given circumstances. Freeing the voice enables the actor to connect with his scene partners and his audience in a genuine and honest way.

Voice Training Helps the Actor to Authentically Create Character

Actors will often be called upon to become people who are drastically different from themselves. An actor playing Dot in *Sunday in the Park with George* will need to learn how to sound like a young woman in Act I and a very old woman in Act II. An actor in a Sam Shepherd play may need to learn how to sound tougher and rougher around the edges than he really is. A Brian Friel play or a Tennessee Williams play often demands that an actor learn how to authentically sound as if he is from a different part of the world.

Whether expressing age, class, or region, the minute an actor is vocally inauthentic on stage is the moment that he loses credibility and loses the audience's faith. How many times have you heard a bad British dialect in a play and not been able to buy anything that the characters were going through as being authentic and truthful? (If I had a dime for every time, I'd have a Mercedes by now!) Voice training helps the actor to learn the tools that he needs to master the creation of character and the development of an authentic dialect.

What Do All Vocal Training Models Have in Common?

If you are entering a graduate acting program, vocal training will play an important role in your development as an actor. If you are piecing together your training from various sources, vocal and movement training should be as much a part of your menu for professional growth as acting training.

That said, there are many different schools of thought and many different vocal training models. We'll talk about the biggies in a minute. Although each school of thought has its own ways of articulating the mechanics of voice as well as its own distinct training and development exercises, their aims are pretty much the same.

The aim of all vocal training methodologies is to help the actor return to a neutral state, free of habit and the encumbrances of adult life, so that his vocal instrument may become as free and unfettered as possible.

If you think about it, using your voice effectively is really not all that complicated. As babies we all instinctively knew how to use our voices to communicate optimally. The piercing shriek of a distressed infant on an airplane will confirm this. With their voices babies easily transmit their pleasures and their discomforts to those around them. They use their voices so fully that they dominate any room that they are in. Their voices are present and powerful. Little kids do this, too. This is why they are told to use their "inside voices." Children have resonant, clear, and healthy vocal instruments.

It is only as we get older, as we become burdened by the tensions of life and by the endless self-consciousness and self-monitoring and self-obfuscating that we all do, that our vocal presence becomes muddied and murky. As our self-consciousness grows, we censor and tamp down our innate ability to express the needs, desires, and requirements at the core of our being. Our true selves become submerged under the false exteriors we are often conditioned to display as we grow into adulthood.

Just as a baby's voice commands the attention of anyone in its presence, an actor's voice must command the presence of an audience. It is therefore the goal of all vocal training to strip away the layers of tension and self-consciousness that life has saddled us with to achieve the freedom that we knew earlier in our lives. Only then, when we peel off these layers of artifice, stress, and habit, will we communicate as freely, simply, effectively, and truthfully as we once did.

Different vocal training methods have this idea in common: the voice is the body. Actors often come into vocal training thinking that their voice is some small mechanism located in their throat when, in fact, the entire body is a resonator for sound like the giant pipes of an organ in a cathedral. A rich, full sound requires a rich, full breath, and the foundation for this is in the low, deep part of the abdomen, the body's core or center. The body's center is locus and the core of all that is primal and truthful. In the moments of our greatest vocal sincerity we still know how to access this place.

In short, all vocal training methods, no matter the vocabulary or the imagery that they use, help the actor to achieve a full and relaxed breath and aid him in accessing his body. Once the actor connects the voice to the breath and the body, he can begin to strip away the layers of tension and habit that have accumulated over the course of a lifetime so that he can return, as much as possible, to a state of vocal and physical neutrality. Only from a state of relaxed neutrality can the actor begin to find full vocal expression and create a clean canvas from which to build character.

Different Vocal Training Models

The two most common vocal training methods in use in the US today are Fitzmaurice Voicework (which has gained enormous popularity in the past ten years) and Linklater Voice training. Although these two methods seem to be the most prevalent in American university training programs today, they certainly aren't the only training methods and often borrow ideas and exercises from other methods and practitioners. We'll take a look at the basics of each model.

FITZMAURICE VOICEWORK

If you walk into a Fitzmaurice Voicework class, at best you may think that you've mistakenly entered a yoga studio; at worst you may think that you've mistakenly joined a strange cult. You will see many actors with their legs in the air shaking them, or rather, being shaken by them, and making strange vocal sounds while doing this. It may seem strange, bizarre, weird, perhaps even certifiable to the casual observer, but it works!

Catherine Fitzmaurice is the mastermind behind Fitzmaurice Voice-work. A natural healer, Fitzmaurice has drawn on yoga, Reiki, shiatsu, and other modalities of healing to unlock the breath and free the voice. Fitzmaurice's basic idea is a pretty simple one: if you can't breathe well, you can't speak well. If breathing is freed, the voice becomes free. It's really that simple. Her entire training system is constructed around this principle (Vocal Yoga).

How does it work? Fitzmaurice work seeks out places in the body where the breath is locked and unlocks it. The first phase of Fitzmaurice work is called **destructuring**. In the destructuring phase, the actor develops a more acute awareness of the body and releases tension through **tremoring**. Tremoring is pretty much what it sounds like. Through a series of yoga-like poses the body is stretched into positions where it (for want of a better way of explaining it) starts to kind of freak out. When it gets freaked out in these weird yoga-like positions, it starts to shake. This shaking sounds like a bad thing, but it's actually a good thing and the aim of tremoring. Once the actor begins to tremor, she is encouraged to release sound from the voice into the tremor. The result is a quaking body and an accompanying quaking voice.

The bulk of my training in Fitzmaurice work focused on this initial destructuring phase. Eventually, the actor moves from destructuring to the next phase, **restructuring**. During restructuring the voice, now freed through tremoring, is retrained. Fitzmaurice work utilizes exercises from the bel canto school of singing to help the actor to learn how to breathe and support the voice more optimally. These exercises help the actor to retrain her muscles in order to breathe fully, efficiently, and without strain. Through repeated use of these exercises, the voice begins to work more efficiently, allowing the actor to focus on acting choices rather than thinking technically about the voice and breath.

This all may sound strange (and it all may look even stranger), but it works. Tremoring really does free the breath and the voice, deepening vocal resonance and moving the breath lower in the body. The result is a much freer and more resonant voice with greater range and flexibility.

Fitzmaurice Voicework is both fast and slow. In terms of overturning years of vocal habit, it is pretty quick and efficient, and yet, to the actor, it may feel like a slow, arduous, or confusing process. Oftentimes the principles of Fitzmaurice work are not explained to the actor who is learning it. In my case, I was launched into the exercises without explanation of what exactly I was doing and why (this is the case for many actors that I know who begin the training). It was only after several weeks of puzzling, bewildering work that I began to understand what I was doing. Then, as I began to see some pretty big changes, I became a fan.

Many actors, like me, may find themselves resistant at first since Fitzmaurice work can feel quite strange initially, but in time grow to love it. For others who find it difficult to tremor, it may not be the best system (in my experience, professional dancers who are incredibly flexible in their limbs and tightly bound at their core have difficulty tremoring). Fitzmaurice may not be the only vocal training tool that you need, but it may be a helpful one. It is the hottest training around right now, so you are very likely to encounter it in one form or another as you continue your actor training.

Programs that currently focus on Fitzmaurice work are the American Repertory Theatre Institute for Advanced Theatre Training at Harvard University, the Yale School of Drama, and NYU. The list is sure to grow more and more over the years as a greater number of voice trainers become certified in the technique.

LINKLATER VOICE

Before Fitzmaurice Voicework became so wildly popular, there was Linklater Voice training. It is a strange phenomenon that I don't fully understand, but you are not terribly likely to find these two training modalities existing side by side. Fitzmaurice people tend not to like Linklater training, and vice versa. It is usually (although not always) an either/or training proposition.

The core idea of the Linklater Voice method is to free the natural voice. If the voice is permitted to find its freest and truest form of expression, the actor will be able to communicate fully on stage.

174

Kristin Linklater developed this vocal training method. She is a dialect coach, actor, director, and teacher of voice and acting, currently on faculty at Columbia University. Linklater believes that everyone has a vocal instrument that is capable of great expression, and that every human voice is capable of navigating through a two- to four-octave pitch range. Without training we only use a small portion of this range, but we are all capable of developing the tools to access the full, natural voice.

Linklater believes that we each have a unique and authentic voice; a sound that is uniquely ours. If that distinct voice is freed, she believes, the true self can be revealed. Through her exercises, the actor will learn to find his true voice—not a good, generic kind of stage voice, but something that is uniquely his.

The work follows a series of exercises. The first portion of the work, much like Fitzmaurice's idea of restructuring, is designed to help the actor to relearn how to breathe naturally. The next portion of training increases breath capacity. Work on vocal resonance is added. In the final stages of work, the actor focuses on language and articulation.

There are many fans of the Linklater method. I have known many actors who, after studying this method in depth, found access to a vocal range that they never knew they had. The work on the breath not only makes the voice fuller and more resonant, but enables the actor to become better connected to language, to the body and even to her own thoughts.

The training to become a certified Linklater teacher is rigorous and demanding and requires an extensive background as an actor even prior to training. The selective nature of the certification process is, I feel, one of its strengths, keeping integrity and continuity in the training.

Linklater training is very popular in American universities. Chances are, if the vocal component of a training program is not Fitzmaurice-based, it will be Linklater-based. Linklater training, obviously, is the offering at Columbia University, where Kristin Linklater teaches. Shakespeare & Company, which Linklater was instrumental in founding, offers professional actor training and draws heavily from her work.

To learn more about Linklater and her ideas, you might start by reading *Freeing the Natural Voice: Imagery and Art in the Practice of Voice and Language*, by Kristin Linklater and Andre Slob.

Linklater vocal training would serve nearly any actor well, and might be especially helpful for actors who feel as though they are not able to fully connect with their breath or those who feel in some way out of tune with their true selves. Actors who may not respond as favorably might be actors who learn in a more concrete way and do not respond to imagery quite as well. Like any training method, or like eating calamari or brussels sprouts, you won't know if you like it until you try it.

LESSAC TRAINING

Sadly, in 2011 the world of voice training lost the 101-year-old Arthur Lessac, creator of Lessac Kinesensic Training for the voice and body. The goal of Lessac training is like the other vocal training methodologies that we've looked at in that its aim is to free to voice and body from habitual tensions, but its path to this goal is quite different. Lessac training does not utilize imagery or any kind of exterior elements to train the voice; rather the student experiences the physical production of sound as vibration. Lessac master teacher Nancy Krebs explains:

> It is a sensory approach, feeling the dynamics of energy, vibration or muscular action. "Kinesensic" is a term that Arthur coined from *kine* for movement, *esens* for basic meaning, nature; *sens* for spirit, inner energy, and *sic* for familiar occurrences. So this training teaches the individual to feel and recognize the sensations of voice production, and to allow those sensations to guide the process of becoming vocally and physically "aware." It is gentle, enjoyable, reliable, and extremely comprehensive, covering all aspects of voice and speech, while relaxing and energizing the body at the same time. (Krebs)

Lessac defined three vocal energy states: **consonant**, **tonal**, and **structural**.

- Consonant energy: Every consonant is assigned an equivalent orchestral instrument that best describes or approximates its particular vibration. These consonant instruments have distinct tonal and melodic qualities that distinguish them. Lessac termed this the **consonant energy orchestra**.

- Tonal energy: To help students understand how sound waves vibrate through the bones of the head and internal jaw and mouth structure, Lessac uses a humming vowel sound that he calls the **Y buzz**. A kind of vocal panacea, it grounds the voice, helps the actor find resonance, and can even help a strained voice to heal.

- Structural energy: Understanding the optimal space she must create in the mouth for all speaking and singing sounds helps the actor to enhance tonal quality in all produced sounds.

To gain a greater understanding of Lessac's work, you may want to read *The Use and Training of the Human Voice: A Bio-Dynamic Approach to Vocal Life.* You can also learn more about Lessac training at www.lessacinstitute. com.

Lessac training today is not quite as prevalent in America as Linklater or Fitzmaurice training. It is difficult to pinpoint exactly why. It may be because Lessac was so particular about the teachers that he trained that there simply are not that many Lessac instructors around. For the actor who does not connect with imagery, but rather seeks a kinesthetic experience to understand sound, Lessac training might be a good route.

PATSY RODENBURG AND CICELY BERRY

Two last vocal trainers bear mentioning in our discussion here. While they do not have their own training methodologies with a capital "T," or certification programs to pass along their wisdom and ideas to a next generation of teachers, both are superlative coaches of voice whose ideas you are bound, during your training, to bump into.

Patsy Rodenburg is the director of voice at the Royal National Theatre, teaches at the Michael Howard Studio in New York, and is one of the world's leading voice teachers and coaches. Her work is incredibly practical and accessible, with techniques that help the actor to free physical tensions, opening up the voice and centering the body. Her unique focus is on energy and stage presence. She has a particularly useful and enlightening way of viewing stage energy (which translates to vocal and physical energy in performance). In your training you might encounter Rodenburg's energy exercises. You may also be interested in her very insightful book *The Second Circle.* Other books are *The Right to Speak* and *The Actor Speaks.*

Cicely Berry is the vocal director of the Royal Shakespeare Company. Like all vocal trainers, she is interested in the free and open voice. Her primary lens is language. She seeks to help actors to understand the power of language and how language, when its full power is truly harnessed, has the capacity to stir the soul. In your training you may encounter text exercises from Cicely Berry, particularly when approaching Shakespeare and heightened texts. Her books include *Voice and the Actor, The Actor and the Text,* and *Text in Action.*

Vocal Training Methods: What Is Best?

I have touched on some of the most prevalent vocal training methods here, but this discussion is not by any means all-inclusive. There are many people who have many valid ideas about vocal training. These practitioners just happened to have ideas that somehow caught fire and became recognized and popular. Much like actor training, all vocal training methods have similar ideas and aims, but systems of delivery and terminology vary. What rocks one actor's world can leave another actor cold, confused, bewildered, or turned off. Visit classes. Read the suggested books. Try to figure out which system might resonate best with your particular vocal challenges, or, if you do not yet know what your challenges are, which way of thinking and experiencing seems to fit best with your personality and way of working. My best advice is to try to stay open no matter what the training is like. A system that at first blush may feel strange, alien, or nonsensical just might ultimately be the system that will change you and your vocal instrument the most.

Demystifying Physical Acting Training

As we said in the Vocal Training Methods section, the actor's instrument is his voice and body. It should come as no surprise then that the body, just like the voice, needs to be rigorously trained and developed.

All actors need to cultivate a flexible and sensitive body so that they can pursue action on stage. I would argue that this is especially true for American actors. Sad to say, but we are a society that is becoming more and more disconnected from our bodies. Having taught in Eastern and Central Europe, in the UK, and in Asia, I can say that we are more cut off from our bodies and from our impulses as a culture than other cultures are. I can't quite tell you why. It could be our increasing conversation with technology rather than with each other. It could be the role of food and exercise in our culture. It could be our sedentary lifestyle, due to our dependence on cars rather than on walking and bike riding. A sociologist would have a better idea about this than I do. Whatever the reason, we are, as a whole, rather cut off from ourselves.

As an actor who was very physically cut off myself, I understand the need for training all too well (I once had a director tell me that I was a "brilliant actor . . . from the neck up." I was so young that I thought it was a compliment, not a criticism). When you are a physically challenged actor as I was (and still, to some degree, am) you may find yourself trying on many different training methods until you find one that truly resonates with you.

Why Do Actors Need Physical Training?

Quite simply, when you are cut off from your body, you are cut off from your impulses. Have you ever seen an actor on stage who was rigid, clenched, locked down, and "muscling up" his energy? This is an actor who isn't physically free. When an actor isn't physically free, the audience recognizes that he is an actor acting, rather than believing that he is the character. When the actor's body is tense on stage, the work is tense and effortful. When the work is effortful and when the actor's impulses aren't honored, the work becomes untruthful. Theatre is all about the revelation of the truth, creating the illusion of truth on stage, and living truthfully under imaginary circumstances. If the actor cannot be free enough to be truthful, he cannot truly act on stage.

In addition to this, to create character demands not only freedom in the body, but the ability to understand other people's physical habits and limitations. One of the goals of all physical acting training is to bring the actor to a kind of "physical neutral," a state where she can strip away all of her habitual tensions. Once the actor understands how to bring her own body to neutral, she can then layer other people's habits and physical characteristics on her blank canvas. The actor must strip away her own physical habits so that she can take on the habits of her character. For example, an actor playing an older character will need to assume the physical characteristics of aging. If this means playing a character with rounded shoulders and a slightly collapsed lower back who shuffles her feet when she walks, the actor will need to start from as physically neutral a place as possible in order to take these physical characteristics on. If she doesn't know how to strip away her own physical habits—her way of moving, her habitual mode of storing physical tension—she will not be able to truthfully inhabit another character.

We've touched on physical acting training in this book already in the chapters on Grotowski, Suzuki, and others. Where is the separation between "physical acting training" and "acting training"? Well, really, there shouldn't be a separation. It is all part and parcel of the same craft, and the same actor's body, mind, and spirit engaging in this craft. For example, Viewpoints work is a system of actor training and rehearsal, and yet, for this actor, it was more enlightening and freeing physical acting training than any other method. Fitzmaurice work is called "voice work," and yet, because of its yoga-like component, it is as physical as any physical acting training method. All of these training components work hand in hand to strengthen and free the actor mentally and physically. The training models and techniques that I am about to describe have long been categorized by theatre trainers as physical disciplines of acting and, in your training, will come under the heading of "movement for the actor."

Different Physical Training Models

ALEXANDER TECHNIQUE

Once upon a time an Australian actor named F. M. Alexander suffered from repeating laryngitis. Doctors could not find an explanation or a way to help him. Alexander, frustrated, got to work solving his own problem. He realized that tension in his neck and his body was the culprit. An inefficient use of his body was putting unnecessary pressure on his voice to the point where he was damaging it. He developed a way of moving with greater ease and efficiency that reduced the pressure on his neck. His health improved, his voice became stronger, and his laryngitis went away. This was the beginning of the Alexander Technique, which Alexander continued to refine and later passed on to other teachers.

The Alexander Technique is a tool to help people move with greater ease and flexibility. It is used in acting training very frequently, though the technique is by no means limited to actors and is used by all kinds of people in all kinds of professions who want to change the way they move. Alexander Technique can help to alleviate chronic pain or correct poor posture. For the actor, it can be an incredibly useful tool to strip away habit, reduce tensions, and bring the body back to a point of neutrality. The Alexander Technique website explains it this way:

We all have unconscious movement habits. Without realizing it, we put undue pressure on ourselves. We use more force than we need to lift a coffeepot or a weight bar. We slouch as we sit, unaware that our way of doing things gives our bodies a certain look. We blame body problems on activities—carpal tunnel syndrome on computer work, tennis elbow on tennis. But often it is how we do something that creates the problem, not the activity itself.

An Alexander Technique teacher helps you see what in your movement style contributes to your recurring difficulties—whether it's a bad back, neck and shoulder pain, restricted breathing, perpetual exhaustion, or limitations in performing a task or sport. Analyzing your whole movement pattern—not just your symptom—the teacher alerts you to habits of compression in your characteristic way of sitting, standing, and walking. He or she then guides you—with words and a gentle, encouraging touch—to move in a freer, more integrated way (Alexander Technique Nebraska and Toronto).

The core principle of the Alexander Technique is that in order to achieve freedom and flexibility in the body, the head and neck must be free. If the muscles of the neck are relaxed and free, the head balances lightly and fluidly on top of the spine. If the neck is relaxed and the head is balancing on the spine, the entire body releases. In a way, this is kind of the reverse of Suzuki training. Suzuki, you'll recall, is all about the actor feeling the connection of the feet to the ground. Once the connection to the ground is established, the upper body achieves a kind of fluidity. In Suzuki, the awareness is drawn to the feet and fluidity comes through the rest of the body as a result of this focus. Alexander Training is something of an opposite process—top-down instead of bottom up. Fluidity and freedom in the head and neck trickle down to create freedom and flexibility through the rest of the body.

In Alexander training you will be asked to observe your own patterns of movement. Often you are called upon to move the way you might move during the course of the day. You might lie down, sit down, or walk across the room and observe how you are doing this, what muscles you are engaging and where you are holding tension. Your teacher may assist you in doing this by making physical contact with you to make you aware of your movement patterns and help you to understand where you are storing tension.

To benefit from Alexander Technique, the actor cannot just think about her movement while in class doing the exercises, but needs to bring awareness to her movement in daily life. How does she use her body to take out the garbage, scoop the cat box, and make toast? While she is performing these tasks in every day life, what adjustments can she make to make her movement more efficient? It is a 24/7 commitment to change. It is a slow and steady process of stripping away habitual tensions.

Because it is such a slow and gentle process, Alexander Technique requires a great deal of patience. The results are subtle and gradual, unfolding very slowly over time. Our American love of instant gratification won't really work here. As a young actor I didn't get it. Lying on an exercise mat thinking of my head and neck being free wasn't doing it for me. I was punchy and impatient. I remember being in a New York acting studio in an Alexander class walking across the room, supposedly noting how I was engaging my body, when I was really thinking about Thai food. I couldn't focus. I didn't get it and I didn't change.

Five years later, as a more serious actor, in a location where the Thai food wasn't quite as good, I got it. I dedicated myself to the process, and through the help of a very gifted teacher, amazing things started to happen. My turned-out feet became neutral. My posture improved. My body reorganized itself.

Alexander training is a powerful tool for bringing the body to neutral. As my colleague, movement teacher and director Jana Tift, explained to me,

> To me, Alexander Technique is an essential study for actors, because it awakens body and movement awareness, which makes it possible to identify and let go of limiting movement habits, like hunching the shoulders or thrusting the head forward. With the body in balance,

actors can access a whole array of movement choices, authentic choices that serve the character and the play. They are freed from their habitual tension, and they are delighted to discover that their bodies respond easily to organic impulse and genuine emotion. AT (Alexander Technique) gives the actor a big gift: an authentic presence onstage.

It should be noted that Alexander Training is as much a way of thinking and being as it is a method of physical understanding. Dancer, choreographer, and movement teacher Toni Poll-Sorenson explained it to me this way:

> My love of AT (Alexander Technique) comes from the freedom it provides, not just in movement, but in my thinking. All of what we do in the arts, whether dance or theater or music, is so complex. The complexity can get in the way. Dance isn't about the steps, music isn't about the notes on the page, and acting isn't about the lines or the blocking. We must do all that, but within an awareness that is unconsciously self-aware and honest/authentic. If I am using my body well, I only have to notice when I pull down . . . I don't have to attend to every little thing. I don't have to posture and preen.

Alexander Technique provides actors with a way of truly inhabiting their own bodies. It is probably the most common physical acting training thread in actor training programs in America. For those who dedicate themselves to this process, the results can be quite dramatic. The actor can gain a much greater sense of how the body works and thereby learn to allow the body to work more efficiently. Once good habits are learned, the aware body likes to hang on to these efficient habits. Take it from the lady who doesn't walk like a duck with turned-out feet anymore. Thanks, F. M. Alexander.

LABAN MOVEMENT ANALYSIS (LMA)
Laban Movement Analysis is another method of physical acting training.

It is not a system of training unto itself, but rather is a vocabulary, a way of describing and understanding movement. Laban Movement Analysis is sometimes called Laban/Bartenieff Movement Studies. Bartenieff Fundamentals, the work of dancer and physical therapist Irmgard Bartenieff, are a component of Laban training and are a means of describing body patterning and connectivity. You may encounter the name of this movement analysis tool under either title, but it is the same tool.

Developed by pioneering choreographer and student of human movement Rudolph Laban, Laban Movement Analysis is a multidisciplinary approach. It draws from the study of human psychology as well as anatomy and other interrelated fields. Laban Movement Analysis looks for patterns in human movement, describing the ways we move, our patterns of movement, and our relationship to space.

Laban Movement Categories

Laban breaks down movement analysis into these categories:

- **EFFORT.** Effort means understanding and identifying the way the body uses energy to mobilize itself; in short, how we move.
- **SPATIAL ACCESS.** This category looks at where we go in space and why.
- **BODY CONNECTIVITIES (BARTENIEFF FUNDAMENTALS).** What parts of the body move and what parts of the body help to balance and stabilize the actor?
- **SHAPING QUALITIES.** This category investigates the way that movement is shaped and patterned. It looks at how we habitually like to do things and how we like to move (Connected Movement).

Laban Movement Analysis is used not only in the arts, but also in health rehabilitation and other disciplines. Laban's capacity for describing movement is very expansive. Although it is only one component of Laban Movement Analysis, the idea of **effort** is perhaps the most focused-on aspect in acting training.

The Laban efforts, as we said, describe how the body moves. Laban Analysis looks at particular kinds and qualities of effort (there are eight movement efforts, which we will identify in a minute) and at **weight**, **time**, **space**, and the **flow** with which an effort of movement is pursued. Let's first look a little more closely at weight, time, space and flow and define them:

- **WEIGHT: STRONG OR LIGHT.** How the actor directs his weight. Does he move with a quality of lightness or heaviness in his movement?
- **TIME: SUSTAINED OR QUICK.** Is time broken up (quick) or does the actor move through time in an expansive manner (sustained)?
- **SPACE: DIRECT OR INDIRECT.** Does the actor move through space directly? Or does the actor wander through space indirectly?
- **FLOW: BOUND OR FREE.** Does the actor move with fluidity in a free manner, or is his movement bound and controlled?

Laban identifies eight movement efforts. Each of these efforts uses a combination of the qualities listed above. Each movement effort has a different combination of quality of weight, time, space, and flow. Here are the eight basic efforts:

- **FLICKING:** A light, quick, indirect movement (think of flicking a piece of lint off of your sweater)
- **WRINGING:** A strong, sustained, indirect movement (think of wringing out a wet wash rag, although this movement certainly is not limited to being expressed through and by the hands)

- **DABBING:** A light, quick, direct movement (think of dabbing a paint brush onto a canvas)
- **PUNCHING:** A strong, quick, direct movement (think of kicking a punching bag)
- **FLOATING:** A light, sustained, indirect movement (think of floating on water or floating in outer space)
- **SLASHING:** A strong, quick, indirect movement (think of ripping a knife through a canvas)
- **GLIDING:** A light, direct, sustained movement (think about ice skating on a pond)
- **PRESSING:** A strong, direct, sustained movement (think about trying to close your overstuffed suitcase with your elbow)

Wait. What does this have to do with being an actor? Well, as we know, different people have different habitual ways of moving. The eight movement efforts are yet another tool for understanding the movement of self and the movement of character. Different personalities and circumstances bring about different kinds of movement. A thin, calm person may tend to use movements that are light, direct, and sustained in quality, while a heavier person under duress might engage in movement patterns that are more strong, direct, and quick. Look at the above efforts. Which ones do you think you use most often? (On most days, I'm a dabber for sure . . .) These patterns of movement might change with shifts in the person's circumstances or emotional state. I think that you can begin to see how understanding these different patterns and qualities of movement not only help the actor to understand her own habitual movements, but could be an invaluable tool in the understanding and creation of character. I once again turn to movement practitioner Toni Poll-Sorenson:

> Laban gives me a strategy for understanding others . . . judging space
> and time in relationship. It also helps me in character analysis . . . each

person has inherent tempo to their movement . . . each person occu-
pies space uniquely and relates to others uniquely. Laban helps me to
find those different ways of expressing a new character.

Laban can have even broader applications. As a teacher of Shakespeare
text, I often have my students apply Laban movement efforts to the
inherent qualities of consonant sound in the text (I am not unique in
this approach, many teachers do this). My students move through the
text physically, speaking the text while focusing on a Laban movement
effort that seems to encapsulate the specific quality of the texts' sounds
and meaning. So, Laban is not only a means for understanding one's own
pattern of movement, but an entryway for the actor into the character's
psychology and the inherent psychology of words and sound. This is a
pretty powerful tool for the actor that can address so much more than
movement itself.

LECOQ

Jacques Lecoq is perhaps the most influential teacher of physical acting for the theatre. French-born Lecoq had an interest in exploring all
forms of movement, including dance, gymnastics, and mime. He studied
mime with Jean Daste (where he came to understand mask work in performance and the principles of Japanese Noh theatre). He later worked in
Germany and Italy. While in Italy he fell in love with commedia dell'arte,
a form of theatrical comedy prevalent in Italy in the sixteenth century,
involving masked characters. He also experimented with masked ancient
Greek tragedy. In short, Lecoq loved movement and found ancient forms
of movement especially powerful. In the mid-1950s, he opened his own
school for the study of physical theatre, the École Internationale de Mime
et de Théàtre in Paris (The Academy Literature and Drama Website).

Lecoq's work in physical acting cannot be separated from the times
in which he lived. Having survived the devastation of World War II, he
saw theatre as a way of rebuilding a struggling country and returning a

sense of power to people who had been ravaged by the war. He sought to create a kind of theatre that would bridge the distance between people and would speak to people across cultures and social classes. His desire to find a universal means of communication explains his fascination with all aspects of physical storytelling. Lecoq's interest was not in the text, but in what could be communicated through the actor's body.

Lecoq believed that a physical movement could generate or communicate an emotional state, and believed that actors needed to start with the movement and allow it to lead them towards an emotion, rather than generate an emotion and have a movement accompany it. He believed that entire stories could be told physically, without dialogue. His emphasis was on the tension that existed in space between people. He also believed in the importance of working as an ensemble, rather than as a solo actor. This is not a surprise given that his primary influences—Noh theatre, commedia dell'arte and ancient Greek choral work—all emphasized ensemble.

Let's take a look again at the list of theatrical forms that I just named. What else do all of these forms of theatre—Noh theatre, commedia dell'arte, and ancient Greek choral work—have in common? The answer: masked actors. Lecoq was fascinated by mask work. He valued simplicity and practicality and was particularly drawn to masks because they were a simple and direct way to transform the actor.

Here is the beauty of all mask work; without the ability to express emotion through the face (which is obscured by the mask), the actor must use the entire body to convey thought and emotion. Lecoq believed that when an actor goes to put on a mask for the first time, he must study it and, with a kind of respect and reverence, accept what that mask has to give him. There is a freedom in accepting the mask as the actor temporarily leaves behind self and identity. It was Lecoq's work with masks that, if you pardon my play on words, "unmasked" mask work for the contemporary theatre. Older theatrical forms, like commedia and Noh, gained a modern resonance through his work.

Lecoq's training methods helped actors to release preconditioned views of acting and brought their attention back to a sense of playfulness. In his work, the actor's imagination and playfulness is meant, ultimately, to engage the playfulness of the audience. Lecoq felt that through a strong, ensemble-driven creative process, his actors would become free and open communicators within their bodies. This sense of freedom would affect the audience, transcending language and speaking universally to all audience members, regardless of their spoken language, belief system, or political opinions. He sought to create a universal experience that would diminish the separation between the actor and the audience and unite people across cultures.

Lecoq is often included in American theatre training as part of a movement curriculum that will most likely have other components and influences. Actors studying Lecoq will find a strong improvisational experience as well as an immersive ensemble experience.

While you are likely to be exposed to some element of Lecoq work in graduate training, you can also find many workshops that offer an introduction or a more immersive experience. Movement Theater Studio NYC holds a range of Lecoq, clown, and mask workshops (www.movementtheaterstudio.com). The Dell'Arte International School of Physical Theatre in Blue Lake, California, offers a yearlong course including a substantial Lecoq component taught by one of Lecoq's students (www.dellarte.com). Or, for the completely immersive experience, you could attend Lecoq's school, École Internationale de Théâtre Jacques Lecoq, in Paris (www.ecole-jacqueslecoq.com). You could get life-changing training and some pretty amazing croissants.

Lecoq training is a marvelous tool for any actor and is especially beneficial for the actor who has forgotten how to play. Unlocking the physical self and allowing the body to tell stories, and to drive that storytelling rather than relying solely on the mind or the text, is a gift for any actor. For, as Lecoq once said, "The body knows things about which the mind is ignorant."

MEYERHOLD

Once again, we butt up against a head-scratcher of a tricky question: should this next great theatre thinker be mentioned in a conversation about movement disciplines, or one about acting disciplines; or is he really a theoretician? I am speaking now of the work of Russian-born theatre practitioner Vsevolod Meyerhold, who approached theatre in an entirely kinesthetic way. Meyerhold's work could have been included among the acting training methods, just as Suzuki's work and Grotowski's work could have appeared here in the physical training chapter. I am including Meyerhold in a discussion of physical theatre and movement because, unlike Suzuki, who believes in the power of language, and unlike Grotowski, who sought to create his own theatrical language, Meyerhold was completely disinterested in text and language; his true concern was for the actor's movement. Although Meyerhold's work and ideas do not get a great deal of named focus in American acting training, he nonetheless was an enormously important theatrical innovator whose ideas have had far-reaching affects on our theatrical consciousness.

Meyerhold was an actor and director living at the same time as Stanislavsky and Anton Chekhov. Meyerhold was not interested in text or psychology, as were his Russian contemporaries. Rather, it was the visual spectacle of theatre that fascinated him. He was disdainful of theatrical realism, and thought that the theatre should embrace a kind of heightened and stylized reality. He was interested in theatrical truth, but sought to create a theatre that did not copy or even imitate the reality of everyday life. He instead wanted to help actors to form a different kind of theatre, one that would inspire and elevate its audience by creating a non-naturalistic, anti-illusionistic theatrical experience. What do I mean by an anti-illusionistic theatrical experience? I mean that he wanted his audience to be aware that they were watching actors on a stage, and he wanted his actors to engage the audience, rather than to create the idea that they were separate from them.

To break free from the established conventions of realism and theatrical illusion, Meyerhold turned to a kind of theatre that was entirely physically based. Like Lecoq, Meyerhold investigated mime, acrobatics, commedia dell'arte, Noh, and Kabuki theatre. He formulated an entirely new and revolutionary approach to acting called Biomechanics (The Academy Literature and Drama Website).

Biomechanics focuses on the actor's physical control and balance. It emphasizes his rhythmic awareness and engagement with all external stimuli, including other actors and the environment surrounding them and the audience. In Biomechanics, movement and gesture hold greater power than spoken words.

In Russia in the early 1900s, the symbol for motion was the machine. It was the machine that drove progress in Meyerhold's society. Meyerhold posited that the trained actor was not really all that different from a machine. Machines could execute tasks with great precision, and so could the trained actor.

During Meyerhold's life, there was a great deal of attention being paid to the physical efficiency (or lack thereof) of assembly-line workers. Meyerhold applied the same principles used to study the physical movements of assembly-line workers to studying actors. Just as unnecessary or extraneous movements in the assembly-line workers hindered industrial progress, inefficient movement in actors cluttered stage life, muddied intention, and dulled the power of theatre.

Meyerhold looked for physical efficiency in his actors and for the most effective way to convey meaning on stage. One simple gesture could convey what pages and pages of dialogue or a series of elaborate movements might otherwise be used to communicate. He was interested in sparseness, simplicity, and clarity. The most efficient and effective route to convey meaning to an audience was most often not literal but representational.

Mcyerhold believed that there were basic laws of theatre. Like so many theatre practitioners that would come after him, he sought to create a language for theatre and to identify and understand the elements that made up theatre. He named **movement, space, rhythm, and gesture as** theatre's primary elements.

In Biomechanics, the actor needed to focus on three things. She needed to find her center of balance, she needed to identify an expressive position in space, and she needed to develop an awareness and understanding of rhythm. Through a series of training exercises, Meyerhold's actors developed incredible physical precision in the service of conveying meaning to an audience.

Biomechanics will certainly creep into your training, even if it is not directly named. Meyerhold's work has had a profound effect on theatre greats such as Peter Brook and Bertold Brecht. No doubt his aesthetic and these principles will be present in various components of your study of acting and on your physical acting training.

Biomechanics never really took off in American training the way other methods did. Perhaps this is because it was more like a theatrical experiment and series of ideas than a complete and articulated training system. It was a style of theatre and a way of thinking about theatre that did not get fully disseminated. But perhaps even more significant was the fact that Meyerhold did not write much. Had he written a book or a series of books, as Stanislavsky did, the face of training might look very different today.

PHYSICAL ACTING TRAINING METHODS: WHAT IS BEST?
Just like voice training, the physical acting training that is most effective depends on the individual. The good news is this: in formal programs of study the physical acting training that you will receive is usually a smattering of different methods. Where voice training generally is less of an amalgam (usually voice practitioners are either Linklater practitioners or Fitzmaurice trainers with a side order of some other discipline), physical acting training is fairly eclectic. In a good graduate program, you are likely to get a mix of Alexander, Laban, and some clown and mask work. If some particular aspect of training really resonates with you, there are always ways to pursue that kind of training more fully.

A wonderful resource is the website The Moving Theatre (http:// physicaltheatre.webs.com/schoolsandworkshops.htm). This is a site dedicated to international training in various movement disciplines, including Meyerhold, Grotowski, Laban, and Lecoq. In the US, you will find useful training in physical theatre at respected theatre training programs in universities or at top studios in major cities. The majority of training programs that focus entirely on physical theatre can be found outside of America, with programs in the UK, Germany, and Russia.

16

A Look at Degree-Granting Training Programs

There is really no way to touch on every good training program that is out there. There are many hidden gems and many over-hyped disappointments. Good training, as we have said throughout this book, comes in all kinds of different forms. Sometimes all you need is one fantastic teacher to open up a whole new world for you, and sometimes you will find those teachers in the most unlikely places. As we've also said, all training is valuable training. This section takes a look at some well-known degree granting programs, meaning programs that grant the terminal degree in acting, the MFA

A terminal degree doesn't mean that you die from completing it, like a terminal illness—although actually I think graduate school almost killed me (and many people I know). A terminal degree terminates an academic trajectory; it is the end of the road in degree-land in theatre. If you are a theatre practitioner (one who does theatre and makes theatre, rather than one who writes about theatre in a scholarly sense), the MFA is the degree to have. If you wish to be a theatre historian, the PhD, not the MFA, is needed. You can also teach at a university with an MFA, but if you're pursuing that degree, it's probably because you want to be an actor yourself and aren't yet thinking about a career teaching others.

Unified Auditions—Graduate and Undergraduate Programs)

Remember that unified auditions are a great way to be seen by many prospective degree-granting programs at one time. This can save time and money and may allow you to investigate a program that you might not have looked at much otherwise.

We mentioned the URTA National Unified Auditions earlier in this book (for a list of URTA member schools, visit www.urta.com/Member-Schools). URTA auditions are the primary group auditions for graduate school programs. Some undergraduate programs also attend the URTAs and do their recruiting for BFA programs there. URTA holds auditions in New York, Chicago and San Francisco—though not all schools go to all locations. I personally think the auditions are a little more relaxed and less crazy outside of New York, so if you have a choice of regions, you might consider the calmer pace of the Midwest or California.

If you go to these auditions and are not passed on through their initial screening process, all is not lost. There are other schools in attendance at these meetings who will be happy to meet with you and you should go out and find them instead of licking your wounds. There are all kinds of reasons why actors do not pass a preliminary screening audition. I have seen some really gifted actors not get passed through, and conversely I have seen some really ho-hum ones get passed along. As with anything in this business, if you do not get passed through the screening audition, do not take that as any kind of meaningful reflection on your talent. Forge ahead! Onward! URTA has a set of group auditions for actors who are not passed on to audition for the member schools. You can also wander around the conference center that is hosting URTA and sign up to meet with and audition for different schools on your own. Meeting schools this way is nice because it affords you far more one-on-one time to talk with them and ask questions.

There are also region-specific unified auditions. The South Eastern Theatre Conference (SETC) is a great example. SETC holds group auditions annually, not only for graduate programs, but for some undergradu ate training programs. Visit their website, www.setc.org/auditions.

If you are searching specifically for unified auditions for undergraduate BFA programs, a great resource is the National Unified Auditions Homepage (unifiedauditions.com/new_index.html). This site lists group auditions for undergraduate BFA programs in New York, Chicago, Las Vegas, and Los Angeles, and also lists universities that will have simultaneous auditions for entry into their programs.

Also, if you are seeking an undergraduate degree, do not rule out good BA programs in favor of BFA programs. There are some really wonderful BA programs in theatre at liberal arts colleges out there. If you are a prospective undergraduate looking for programs, visit the schools you are considering and sit in on their theatre classes. I can say with certainty that there are some BA training programs around that rival not only some BFA programs, but even some MFA programs in quality (my current university, San Francisco State, is such a program). BA programs are a different animal in that they are meant to deliver a more comprehensive liberal arts education and will teach you technical aspects of theatre as well as performance craft. For some students, a broad theatre background might be the right way to go. Discount nothing and keep an open mind!

Graduate Training Programs

Here is some information about some of the better-known degree-granting programs out there. It is, of course, not an all-inclusive training list, nor is it a complete picture of the programs that *are* listed. Hopefully this list will give you a good first step and a good place to start as you look into your formal training options. I have chosen these programs for inclusion because they are varied, both in terms of their geography and in terms of the focus and style of their training. I have also selected these programs because they have a solid training reputation among most artists and academics.

A word about these listings: Most of these degree-granting programs do not readily identify a specific training methodology that defines their programs. Once upon a time there were graduate training programs that were all Meisner-based or all Method-based. The trend now is toward eclecticism. Most good training programs seek to offer students a variety of training tools. Often, the kind of voice, movement, or acting training that each program offers shifts as faculty resources change; the nature of the training offered might change depending on the talents and passions of the current faculty members.

Specialized training that is undiluted in a specific training methodology is best found at studios and non-degree-granting programs. If you want to learn Practical Aesthetics Technique, the Atlantic Theatre Company is for you. If you want to learn Strasberg and the Method, go to the Lee Strasberg Film and Theatre Institute. If you want to learn Stella Adler Technique, go to the Stella Adler Studio of Acting. Graduate training is more likely to be a mixed bag than an unadulterated training system. If you are seriously considering attending a program, get more information about the specific voice, movement, and acting training that will be offered during the period of time that you plan to attend.

THE AMERICAN CONSERVATORY THEATER (ACT)
Training Programs/Degrees Offered
MFA in Acting

Areas of Actor Training
American Conservatory Theater's MFA program is closely linked with its Tony Award–winning theater (which is the largest theater company in the San Francisco Bay Area). This is a unique program in that the ACT mainstage forms a foundation for the MFA program. Students perform alongside the artists working at ACT and are involved on a daily basis with one of the nation's premiere regional theatres. Training is eclectic and intensive.

In addition to the MFA program, ACT has other unique educational offerings for actors. Studio ACT is a ten-week actor training course. Students are eligible for college credit after completion. ACT also offers a Summer Training Congress.

If you are a BA student attending college elsewhere but would like a more immersive experience in theatre, ACT also offers a new program called the San Francisco Semester. Like a study-abroad program in the US, the San Francisco Semester offers students the opportunity to take a semester away from their home institution to study with the faculty and guest artists of ACT.

Length of Training

The MFA program is a rigorous three-year program with some of the best teaching artists in the country.

THE AMERICAN REPERTORY THEATRE INSTITUTE FOR ADVANCED THEATRE TRAINING AT HARVARD UNIVERSITY/ MOSCOW ART THEATRE INSTITUTE (ART/MXAT)

The ART Program is unique in that training takes place both in Cambridge, Massachusetts, and in Moscow. The program is under the auspices of Harvard University. Since Harvard, whose focus as an institution is more scholarly than artistic, does not grant the terminal acting degree (the MFA), this program joined forces with the Moscow Art Theatre, meaning that participants of the program are issued a certificate of completion from Harvard University while the actual MFA comes from the Moscow Art Theatre.

Training Programs/Degrees Offered

MFA in acting or voice and speech pedagogy. Over the years, the program has offered training in dramaturgy and directing, though those programs have waxed and waned.

Areas of Actor Training

This program offers a variety of approaches to actor training. Stanislavsky forms the core of training with substantial work from Practical Aesthetics. Voice training is predominantly Fitzmaurice-based. Movement work is eclectic. Due to the influence of its Russian-based faculty, there is a large Grotowski component in movement training. There is substantial training in classical work and heightened text.

Length of Training

Training time is two years plus a summer intensive with faculty of the Moscow Art Theatre in residence in Cambridge, Massachusetts. A residency of about two months takes place in residence in Moscow. An actor showcase is presented upon completion of the program.

The actor who will thrive in this program will be a self-starter who is content to learn many different styles of actor training and synthesize her own craft process. The program provides very solid actor training, but does not emphasize the business of theatre, so actors graduating this program should be go-getters who think creatively about the business side of theatre as well as the craft side.

CALIFORNIA INSTITUTE OF THE ARTS (CALARTS)

Training Programs/Degrees Offered

MFA in acting. CalArts also offers a BFA in acting.

Areas of Actor Training

CalArts emphasizes individual mentoring of its graduate actors. Training is eclectic and focuses on the individual, independent artist and his vision. New works and interdisciplinary projects are emphasized in the training program. This is a very rigorous program that recognizes the changing face of theatre and embraces the affect of media on the art form. Training is tailored to the individual needs of the student.

Critical studies are a vital part of the curriculum. The nature of this program is experimental and progressive.

Length of Training

This is a three-year program. CalArts would be a wonderful fit for the highly imaginative, physical actor who is interested in experimentation and new work. CalArts attends the URTA auditions.

DEPAUL UNIVERSITY

The Theatre School at DePaul

Training Programs/Degrees Offered

MFA in acting, directing, or arts leadership.

DePaul also has a undergraduate conservatory that offers a variety of BFA degrees in all aspects of theatre performance, design, and technical theatre.

Areas of Actor Training

Actor training is eclectic. In the first year, emphasis is given to imagination and the exploration of self. The second year of graduate training focuses on classical texts and the demands of period style. The third year builds the actor's professional profile and business skill set. Voice work is inspired by Lessac and influenced by Berry, Rodenburg, and Linklater. Movement draws from yoga, Pilates, and Grotowski.

Length of Training

This is a three-year program for the student who wants to learn while doing. Each year, the Theatre School mounts a wide variety of productions, giving students ample opportunity to utilize what they are learning in the classroom in performance.

THE GEORGE WASHINGTON UNIVERSITY

The Shakespeare Theatre Company's Academy for Classical Acting (ACA)

The Academy for Classical Acting program (ACA) is directly connected to the Shakespeare Theatre Company. ACA works in conjunction with the George Washington University and is located on their main campus.

Training Programs/Degrees Offered
The program offers an MFA in acting.

Length of Training
This twelve-month program provides complete immersion in Shakespeare. Training areas include text exploration, voice (mainly Linklater and Fitzmaurice), Alexander Technique, mask work, and dramaturgy. Movement training includes rhythmic training and Pilates as well as stage combat (with actor-combatants being Society of American Fight Directors [SAFD] certified at the end of the year). Visiting guest artists provide instruction in other disciplines, such as music in Shakespeare and period styles. The program offers forty-four weeks of studio curriculum, two repertory shows, and a final actor showcase in Washington, DC, and in New York.

The ACA is designed for the classical actor, and for the artist who wants a shorter but intense program. Although the focus is on Shakespeare, diverse training methods are used, which means the actor should be open to a variety of approaches. Participants are often already in the mainstream of their careers. Applicants who are accepted usually have more mature résumés than most graduate students. The average age is typically thirty-three to thirty-six. The program accepts sixteen participants a year. Ideal actors for this program are looking to deepen and advance their skill sets in classical work. In spite of the short time frame, the actor can expect a very thorough training in this unique program.

THE JUILLIARD SCHOOL
Training Programs/Degrees Offered
MFA in acting. Juilliard also offers a BFA in drama.

Areas of Actor Training

Juilliard's first year of graduate training introduces the actors to a very wide range of subjects and influences. Training mixes scene study with text analysis, improv, and movement and voice training. In the first year of training, the actor learns to identify her individual strengths and habits. The second year of training focuses on ensemble, using scenes from Chekhov, Shakespeare, and American drama to strengthen skills in a laboratory setting. The aim of the third year of study is to integrate craft and imagination through fully mounted productions and a series of theatrical master classes.

The Juilliard program is unique in that it offers a fourth year of training that serves as a bridge between graduate study and the professional world. This design allows the actor to get a taste for the demands of working in the profession without the jarring feeling of being kicked out of the grad school nest. It is one of the very few programs to offer such a beneficial transitional year.

Length of Training

This program is four years in duration.

NEW YORK UNIVERSITY (NYU)

Tisch School of the Arts

Training Programs/Degrees Offered

MFA in acting. Tisch also offers a BFA in acting.

Areas of Actor Training

In the first year of graduate study, training focuses on release through play, emphasizing the actor's ability to observe his own habits and behaviors. Students spend time getting to know how their body, voice and imagination change as habitual physical tension is released.

Scene study begins in the second semester of the first year. The second year of training represents the transition from technique to application. Hopefully, students will have stripped away many of the habits with which they entered their training. Actors begin to work together as an ensemble with a shared vocabulary as they move into scene study of contemporary and classical texts.

In the final year of training, the faculty work to tie together all the strands of the training to prepare the actors to enter the professional world.

Length of Training

This is a three-year program for the actor interested in a thorough training from some of the best teachers in the country.

RUTGERS UNIVERSITY
Mason Gross School of the Arts

This program is distinctive in that it offers its students a year-long opportunity to study the classics in London at Shakespeare's Globe Theatre.

Training Programs/Degrees Offered

MFA in acting, directing, playwriting, design, or stage management. A BFA degree in acting is also offered.

Areas of Actor Training

In their first year of graduate training, actors begin intensive training in the Meisner Technique. Michael Chekhov Technique is introduced in the second year of training, while the third year focuses on classical text (and is the year spent in residency at the Old Globe in London). An additional semester is required after the third year to help students make the transition to the professional world.

Length of Training

This program is unique in that it is three and a half years. This is for the student who is interested in working with Meisner and Michael Chekhov

Technique and who would be excited about the opportunity to train at Shakespeare's Globe.

UNIVERSITY OF CALIFORNIA, IRVINE
Training Programs/Degrees Offered

MFA in acting, directing, stage management, scene design, costume design, lighting design, or sound design. UC Irvine also offers a BFA in musical theatre and a BA in drama.

In the first year of the graduate program, actors work primarily on finding a truthful connection to themselves and to their acting partners. In the second year, students move into scene work. Voice training centers around Fitzmaurice Voicework. Speech training follows the techniques of Knight-Thompson Speechwork, a technique developed by UC Irvine faculty. The core of their eclectic movement program is contact improvisation. This is supplemented by work in period dance, music theatre dance, aikido, clowning, stage combat, and corporeal mime.

Length of Training

The graduate program is a three-year program that emphasizes ensemble. The actor who will do best in this program is one who has the combination of artistic drive, intelligence, and emotional maturity that will allow her to work well as an ensemble member.

UNIVERSITY OF CALIFORNIA LOS ANGELES (UCLA)
Training Programs/Degrees Offered

MFA in acting, directing, playwriting, or design. UCLA also offers a BA in theatre.

Areas of Actor Training

This is an interdisciplinary acting program. UCLA's program is unique in that it is housed in the School of Theatre, Film and Television. This means that theatre training is plugged into the future of the art form. In addition to traditional actor training models, this MFA integrates digital media and contemporary technologies.

Training is eclectic and individualized, providing students with skills in a range of styles and genres. Practical production experience is an integral part of the training. Students are encouraged to become "actor-producers" making their own work.

Length of Training

This is a three-year program, great for actors who in addition to studying stage technique want to gain a thorough knowledge of film and television through work experience. This is truly a cutting-edge program.

UNIVERSITY OF CALIFORNIA SAN DIEGO (UCSD)

UCSD is unique in that it has a partnership with the famed La Jolla Playhouse, guaranteeing students a professional residency.

Training Programs/Degrees Offered

MFA in acting, dance theatre, sound design, directing, or playwriting. An undergraduate BA degree in theatre is also available.

Areas of Actor Training

UCSD offers training in a range of styles including Meisner and Stanislavsky.

Movement training incorporates Alexander Technique, dance, and stage combat. Speech is Skinner-based and voice is Linklater-based. Acting training begins with forms of realism, moving to training in verse and classical text, with a final year of training in both modern and postmodern material.

Length of Training

This is a three-year program, offering a unique opportunity for professional residency at a Tony Award–winning theatre.

UNIVERSITY OF DELAWARE

Professional Theatre Training Program (PTTP)

Training Programs/Degrees Offered

MFA in acting or technical production.

The University of Delaware PTTP offers an eclectic training mix. Voice work includes both Fitzmaurice and Linklater, as well as the speech work of Edith Skinner. Movement training includes De Croux, Suzuki, and Rolfing bodywork. The acting program uses a varied mix of influences and training systems.

Length of Training

This is a three-year program. Training is rigorous, classically based, and skill-oriented. The program only accepts one class at a time; once a class has been admitted no other students are accepted until that class has graduated.

The program has a professional theatre company in residence. In the third year of their training, actors work as members of the university's professional theatre company, the Resident Ensemble Players (REP).

This program is for the actor who seeks to focus on the classics. The individualized attention and professional ensemble experience are great assets. Due to the fact that this program only accepts a class every three years the timing is important. Keep track of when Delaware intends to recruit a new incoming MFA class.

UNIVERSITY OF MISSOURI-KANSAS CITY (UMKC)

UMKC's curriculum is flexible and allows for the changing demands of the profession, as well as their faculty and student body. They believe that actors come in many shapes and sizes and that no one career or training goal applies to every student. They teach their classes both in traditional semesters and in short, intensive blocks that allow for concentrated study in a particular area of specialization.

Training Programs/Degrees Offered

MFA in acting, costume design, lighting design, scenic design, sound design, stage management, or technical directing. A BA degree in theatre is also offered.

Areas of Actor Training

This is an eclectic program offering a range of training in working with contemporary and classical texts. Movement training includes commedia, clowning, stage combat, and mask work.

Length of Training

This is a three-year program that mixes craft-building with professional preparation and development.

UNIVERSITY OF SAN DIEGO

The Old Globe

Training Programs/Degrees Offered

MFA in dramatic arts

The University of San Diego graduate program is in collaboration with the world-renowned Old Globe Theatre. The students' work at the Old Globe Theatre forms the foundation of acting training.

Areas of Actor Training

Actor training is an in-depth study of Stanislavsky principles as applied to a wide range of theatrical genres, modern and classical, with a special concentration on Shakespeare, English Restoration, commedia, French neoclassical, and nineteenth- and twentieth-century heightened language plays. Voice work is highly eclectic and is drawn from master teachers Berry, Linklater, Rodenburg, Fitzmaurice, and Lessac, and culminates in vocal processes that are adapted to each student's way of learning. Movement disciplines include yoga, Alexander Technique, Laban analysis, mask work, and stage combat (leading toward SAFD skills proficiency recognition). An original solo performance piece, mentored by a faculty member, is the program's capstone project.

Length of Training

This is a two-year, year-round program. It is for students who want to work rigorously on the classics while working professionally to earn their MFA.

VIRGINIA COMMONWEALTH UNIVERSITY (VCU)
Training Programs/Degrees Offered

MFA in theatre pedagogy. BFA in performance.

The graduate program at VCU is unlike most of the other programs that I have listed here. This is a program designed for those who wish to teach the craft of theatre. The program grants the MFA degree and prepares its students in all aspects of classroom training so that its graduates will be uniquely prepared to enter the world of academia.

Length of Training

The program is individualized and tailored to the individual interests and needs of the student. The curriculum is designed in conjunction with a faculty member; programs of study take between two and three years. The program is a mix of pedagogy and performance and imparts not only the ins and outs of the craft of teaching acting, but how to land a job in the academic job market. This is a unique and specialized program for those seeking careers in teaching theatre.

YALE SCHOOL OF DRAMA
Training Programs/Degrees Offered

MFA in acting, sound design, dramaturgy and dramatic criticism, directing, playwriting, stage management, technical design and production, or theater management.

It is also noteworthy that Yale School of Drama offers a certificate in drama for students who do not hold an accredited undergraduate degree. This is especially helpful for those actors who may have entered the professional world directly in lieu of an undergraduate education.

Areas of Actor Training

Yale's first year begins with a concentration on realism. Second-year work expands the focus into verse drama, with an emphasis on understanding and performing the works of Shakespeare. In the second term of the second year, the work shifts to other writers such as Molière, Shaw, and Wilde. The third year is spent exploring the varied material of contemporary theater. Alexander technique, yoga, stage combat, and singing are included in voice and movement training. Voice work is Fitzmaurice-influenced. Acting work is eclectic, and production opportunities are plentiful.

Length of Training

This is a three-year program for actors seeking eclectic training. Participants can expect thorough training from some of the best teachers in the field.

Undergraduate Training Programs

Here are a few notable undergraduate programs. If you are in the search for a BA or BFA, visit these universities' websites. Do they sound like a fit? Are they in regions where you are interested in living during your training?

BALL STATE UNIVERSITY

Muncie, IN

BFA in acting or musical theatre. Conservatory training with a strong liberal arts core.

BOSTON UNIVERSITY SCHOOL OF THEATRE

Boston, Massachusetts

BFA in theatre arts or acting. Conservatory program. Eclectic and individualized training. Emphasis on musical theatre training.

CARNEGIE MELLON UNIVERSITY SCHOOL OF DRAMA
Pittsburgh, Pennsylvania

BFA in drama with a focus in acting or musical theatre. Very regimented and highly respected training.

CATHOLIC UNIVERSITY OF AMERICA
Washington, DC

BA Emphasis on well-rounded liberal arts education.

ELON UNIVERSITY
Elon, North Carolina

BA in theatre studies. BFA in acting or musical theatre.

Individualized, intensive training and ample production opportunities.

EMERSON COLLEGE
Boston, Massachusetts

BFA in acting or musical theatre

Conservatory training with emphasis on liberal arts background. Focus on professional placement.

UNIVERSITY OF HARTFORD, THE HARTT SCHOOL
West Hartford, Connecticut

BFA in acting or musical theatre

Rigorous training. Ample performance opportunities.

SAN FRANCISCO STATE UNIVERSITY
San Francisco, CA

BA in drama

Training in all areas of theatre performance with an emphasis on the well-rounded theatre artist. Students leaving this program often start their own theatre companies.

SUNY PURCHASE CONSERVATORY OF THEATRE ARTS
Purchase, NY

BFA in acting

Membership in the State University of New York system means that the price tag is a bit lower than those of some other programs. This is a very demanding conservatory program.

SYRACUSE UNIVERSITY SCHOOL OF DRAMA
Syracuse, NY

BFA in acting or musical theatre

Eclectic training. Study abroad opportunities. Affiliation with working Equity theatre.

UNIVERSITY OF MICHIGAN
Ann Arbor, MI

BFA in performance with acting or directing concentration

Rigorous conservatory training with a strong liberal arts foundation, an equal mix of performance and academics.

UNIVERSITY OF MIAMI
Miami, FL

BFA in musical theatre or acting

Intensive pre-professional training with a liberal arts foundation.

UNIVERSITY OF MINNESOTA, DEPARTMENT OF THEATRE ARTS AND DANCE
Minneapolis, MN

BFA in acting

Partnership with the highly respected Guthrie Theatre. Rigorous theatre training with an emphasis on an equally well-rounded liberal arts education.

UNIVERSITY OF NORTH CAROLINA SCHOOL OF THE ARTS
Winston-Salem, NC

BFA in acting. They also offer a high school drama program for twelfth-grade students.

Eclectic conservatory training.

17

A Student Q&A Session

I've hit you with a lot of information about different training systems so that you can be as informed as possible as you chart your training journey as an actor. Knowledge is power, and knowing what is what will hopefully help you to find the kind of training that works the best for you.

That said, I can't anticipate all of your questions and all of the information that you need. So I did the next best thing! I asked my students, past and present, what questions they had about actor training. These really were questions that they asked me (not like the *Glamour* magazine beauty questions, where you just know that the author made them up! "How do I wear unmatched plaid this autumn?") I solicited my current students in my acting classes and my past students via e-mail and Facebook for their questions. Many of them asked the same questions. Maybe some of their questions will be the same as some of yours. So here we go.

Some General Training Questions

Q: *I know that you focus on actor training, but as an actor, does it help you to be trained in other aspects of theatre like lighting and set design, or in other technical aspects?*

A: Absolutely. While technical training does not give you an edge in being accepted to training programs in acting, the more you know about all aspects of theatre, the more aware and employable a citizen of the theatre you can be. When I was a new director I wished that I had known more about lighting design and set design so that I could have had a more effective conversation with my designers.

It is a great idea to get as much experience in all aspects of theatre as you can. You may discover that you have a talent that you didn't know you had. One of my best student actors recently discovered that she loved set design and that she was very good at it. It is always great to know more about every aspect of your craft and to have a broader skill set.

Q: *Is it better to get acting training in a class or to do an internship at a theatre?*

A: An internship is really a kind of training. It is on-the-job training and is of great value. It is a different experience than classroom training. Classroom training is about building your acting tool kit, usually in a safe environment. An internship is about learning quickly on your feet. It does not have the air of safety and exploration that classroom training may have, but what better way to learn how to do a job than to work on that job?

Internships often have a heavy labor component that has nothing to do with acting. You may find yourself sewing in a costume shop, working in a scene shop, or doing publicity for a theatre. Be certain before agreeing to an internship that you fully understand the financial ramifications (do they provide paid or subsidized housing, etc.?), the professional implications (can you earn points towards your equity card?), and the labor involved outside of performance experience. Make certain that it will be a valuable experience in terms of developing your craft and connections, and not just a period of serving as cheap labor for a theatre.

Q: *Should I go to graduate school or a certificate training program right after undergrad, or should I wait?*

A: This is another "it depends" question. I have known actors who went directly from undergrad to grad school and got a great deal out of the experience. They knew what they needed and wanted from their training and they were ready for the challenge. For other actors, they were too green or, frankly, too burned-out from undergrad to fully benefit from the experience. I, for one, am glad that I went to graduate school later on. Had I gone earlier, I would not have known what I needed. It took getting my butt kicked out in the real world to know what I needed to learn and to be ready to learn it. So, it really depends on who you are and what your journey has been like.

Q: *How well do American schools prepare you for a professional career internationally?*

A: This is a tricky question because it is so very broad. My best answer is this: while all training has value and moves you forward as an actor, if you are specifically interested in working in a different country, it may be best to train in that country. Let's say that you have family in a country outside of the US but you identify yourself as an American. Train in the country in which you want to work and live. For example, if I were interested in working as an actor in Russia, it would be best to train as an actor in a Russian program in Russia. That way I could come to understand the specific aesthetic and vocabulary at work in that country. A current student of mine is interested in working in Bollywood films. He is looking into getting his acting training in India instead of in the US. This is the best route for his particular goals.

Country-hopping as an actor is tough. It is hard enough being an American actor in America! Be mindful of language and accent barriers. If you chose to train and work in another country, you will need to work hard to neutralize your regional accent and learn to take on the dialect of the place where you wish to work, otherwise you will have a big barrier to getting hired.

Q: *How do I find out if training classes are legitimate or if they just want to take my money?*

A: Good question. There are lots and lots of acting training classes all over.

Look at the credentials of the instructors teaching the class you want to take. Where have they trained? Where have they worked? How long have they been teaching? Beware of any training that is aimed at "actors and models"; these are usually money-making operations. Also, the training that is aggressively popping up all over the internet is screaming a little too loudly for attention. Good training is available and information about it is easily accessible, but it usually isn't coming at you like an aluminum siding salesman.

Also, training with industry professionals like casting directors can be more about making a buck than about training you. Certainly, going to a few of these kinds of classes to get the perspective of industry professionals can be beneficial; just don't invest your life savings in this kind of training.

Sometimes you really just don't know about the training until you experience it. Trust your gut. Try not to sink too much money into programs or training experiences that you are not sure about. Try to talk to other people who have taken classes at the place that you are interested in. If you are looking at a summer training program (particularly one that is overseas), try to talk to other people who have trained there and ask if they felt that the training was worth the expense.

Q: *I want to get private acting lessons. How can I find a teacher?*
A: You might think about contacting a local, respected theatre or a university or college theatre department near you. Often, people on faculty need some extra cash and will be happy to work with you privately. Actors almost always need cash, and a theatre company may be able to put you in touch with a local actor who takes on students.

Graduate Training and Admissions

Q: *What are grad programs looking for in an actor?*
A: Graduate programs are usually looking to assemble a company of actors. What does this mean? It means that they need a range of actors of different types for their program. Think about it. A graduate program will most

likely draw heavily from this pool of actors to cast its shows. Therefore, they cannot have an entire acting company/graduate class of pretty, young, blonde women. A balance of men and women, young leading lady and leading men types, character types, and various ethnicities will make for a much more interesting graduate training class than an entire class of similar actors. Therefore, it doesn't matter how great a leading guy type you are—if your dream program has already found three actors of this type, they are probably going to need to diversify and find other types of actors for their program.

Graduate programs are also looking for mentally stable, literate, hard-working, pleasant people. Talent is very important, of course, but so is personality. Grad training usually involves a great deal of class togetherness. Think of it like going on a two- or three-year Antarctic expedition. Before a scientific team is chosen for an undertaking like this, the potential team members are tested for mental stability so that they don't, say, eat each other during the long, dark, lonely winter. It's a bit like that. A grad program needs to find people who are mentally stable enough to be good ensemble members day-in and day-out. I personally would rather train a less talented actor who is a delight to work with than a super-talented person who is a pain!

How do you show a potential program that you're this kind of team player? Well, if you interview with a school, be friendly, polite, agreeable, and humble, and try to pick up on the subtle social cues that the auditioners are giving you. Do they want you to stay and chat more, or are they behind schedule and eager to move ahead? Pay attention to their signals like you would in any social situation. Crying, becoming aggressive or defensive in the audition room, or being too chatty and overstaying your welcome in the audition room will all put up red flags to the people working hard to select an incoming graduate class. All of the above examples are things that I actually encountered when I was holding auditions for a graduate program that I worked at. I remember being very interested in an actor's audition, but when I was indicating that it was swell meeting him and that it was time to move along, he just stayed plopped in the chair shooting the breeze with me. A very gifted young actor cried buckets in the interview about her dream to be on the stage. One actor even put "being handsome" under the special skills section of his resume. These are all things that may not have been significant. These actors might have been great to work with—but in our very brief meeting I erred on the side of caution and decided to move along to actors who didn't set off any buzzers in my head. So be friendly, be warm, be funny, be a good listener, be professional, and read the auditioners' signals. Know when it's time to engage with the people you meet, and know when it's time to go. Read their body language; do they seem to want you to shake their hands or stay at a distance? In short, do the job of the actor: listen and respond.

Some very valuable advice that was given to me that I will pass on to you: know your worth. You have something to offer a training program. Training programs need good actors to train: they *want* you to be good. Let me repeat that, because it is so important: they *want* you to be good. No one ever auditioning an actor for a program in the history of mankind sat there thinking, "Gee, I hope this person is really sucky."

So often when we audition as actors we expect that the person auditioning us is just waiting for us to fail. This couldn't be further from the truth. The person auditioning us is hoping that we will succeed. If we are good, it will make their day a whole lot easier! So know that people auditioning you want you to be good. They want to like you. Knowing this made everything easier for me. I hope it makes things easier for you.

Q: *How should I prepare my audition for MFA programs? What are programs looking for?*
A: I will focus my answer on MFA auditions, but much of this advice can also apply to BFA program auditions and other kinds of auditions.

The key to a good audition is to select contrasting pieces that show people who you really are. A lot of actors think that they need to show a vast range or "stretch themselves" in the audition. If you are a twenty-something-year-old actor, now is not the time to be King Lear! Select pieces that are within your playable age range, roles that you could be cast as. Select pieces that you enjoy performing and that you connect to. If you don't have fun doing your pieces, find new ones. You can always tell when an actor is having fun and when the performance is a chore.

Most programs ask to see a contemporary dramatic or comedic piece and a contrasting classical piece, usually a Shakespeare monologue. Even if the program only asks for two monologues, it is a really good idea to have a third monologue ready to go in case they ask to see another piece (as a young actor, I once blew an audition for a top school when they asked to see me do another piece and I didn't have anything else prepared).

Pay attention to time limits. Short and sweet is best. It is always better to come in a little under time than to stay too long at the party. Some schools or group auditions will have time limits. Pay very careful attention to these limits—going over time isn't cool. If need be, cut your monologue down so that it isn't too close to the time limit. You don't want to give a rushed, underdeveloped performance because you are nervous about going over a time limit. If the program doesn't specify a time limit, aim for no more than one minute, thirty seconds for a piece. It is always better to leave them wanting more.

A good audition coach would be of great value in this process. Find one whom you like and trust. If you're getting coaching that doesn't resonate with you, find a new coach. It's a worthwhile investment that can make a big difference.

Q: *How do I find a good monologue for my audition?*
A: A good monologue, like a good man, is hard to find. Here is a list of monologue do's and don'ts that I have assembled over years of watching good ones and bad ones. Keep in mind that this is only my opinion, and that you may find other people with a different opinion. Also keep in mind that these "rules" that I have assembled apply in the vast majority of cases that I have seen, but exceptions do exist.

STAY AWAY FROM MONOLOGUE BOOKS. Monologue books are usually the path of least resistance for actors. It is likely that other actors will have your piece, since they too went to the theatre section at Barnes and Noble to find a monologue.

Monologue books also lead actors into the sexy trap of not reading the play. Not knowing the given circumstances of the play is a really bad idea! You need to know the whole play inside and out to do justice to your monologue.

Instead, find monologues from playwrights that you love, or piece together large chunks of dialogue from a play that you love to create your own monologue. Other actors will not have this same monologue, because you have assembled it from the play yourself. It will also help you to know what the other character that you are talking to in the piece is saying so that your monologue will seem more like a real conversation with another person.

FIND A MONOLOGUE THAT TAKES THE VIEWER ON A JOURNEY AND IS LIKE A SELF-CONTAINED MINI-PLAY, WITH A BEGINNING, MIDDLE, AND END. A good monologue always has a major change/surprise/discovery at the end.

FIND A MONOLOGUE THAT HAS AN ARC, WHERE YOUR CHARACTER IS CHANGED BY THE END OF THE PIECE. In a good monologue the character is not the same at the end as he was at the beginning.

FIND A MONOLOGUE WHERE YOU ARE ACTIVELY ENGAGED WITH ANOTHER CHARACTER OR CHARACTERS AND ARE TRYING DESPERATELY TO CHANGE THEM. People want to see you in relationship to another character—they want to see action and high stakes.

FIND A MONOLOGUE WHERE IT IS PRETTY CLEAR WHAT IS GOING ON. If it is not immediately clear who you're talking to, what the situation is, and what you need, your auditioner may spend your whole audition being puzzled—or, worse, they may just check out.

FIND A MONOLOGUE THAT YOU LIKE TO DO AND THAT IS FUN FOR YOU TO PERFORM. Don't be afraid to take a risk. You have to connect with it and love it for it to work for you.

SETTLED, FOCUSED, HONEST, WACKY, QUIRKY, CHARMING, OR FUNNY WINS THE DAY. Don't cry. Don't yell. And, oh please . . . don't scream. Actors often think that this is showing their capacity for emotional access and intensity. What it is really doing is pushing the auditioners away rather than letting them in. Be energetic and dynamic, but be settled, truthful and open. You want to bring people in to you. You don't want to push them away.

DON'T USE MONOLOGUES THAT YOU OR A FRIEND WROTE, unless your friend is Tony Kushner.

KEEP YOUR MONOLOGUE IN THE PRESENT TENSE. No "When I was five my mother . . ." monologues. Monologues in the past tense can often feel inactive and disengaged.

STAY AWAY FROM WHAT I CALL "STORY MONOLOGUES." These are monologues that are more about telling an elaborate story by recounting events than about trying to change someone else. Every once in a while a story monologue can work, but in general you are so much better off finding a monologue that is an active conversation with another person in the present.

BE WARY OF "I HAD THIS CRAZY DREAM" MONOLOGUES. They are everywhere. And, like the story monologue, they usually aren't terribly active.

BE AFRAID, BE VERY AFRAID, OF THE "ON THE PHONE"
MONOLOGUE (you know, the one where you hold your stretched out fingers
up to your ear and mouth and pretend to have a conversation). I have yet to
see one that wasn't deadly.

NO USE OF IMAGINARY PROPS IN YOUR MONOLOGUE UNLESS
YOU ARE MARCEL MARCEAU. On the flip side of that, don't bring
major props with you either. I once saw an actor bring a beach towel,
tanning lotion, a beach ball, and a sun hat to do her monologue—and the
beach was where she belonged.

PLEASE, OH PLEASE, NO MONOLOGUES ABOUT CRUELTY TO
CHILDREN OR CRUELTY TO ANIMALS. I've seen many of these in my
time. What does this material say about the actor who chose it? Similarly,
no woman-bashing or man-hating monologues or monologues that make
you look like you might be a serial killer. Many actors believe this kind of
material will help them to demonstrate dramatic intensity. However, even
if you are a lovely, wholesome person who was a Boy Scout, went to 4H,
and volunteers at soup kitchens, this kind of monologue will give an auditor
pause about what you are really like.

BE CAUTIOUS OF RACIALLY OR POLITICALLY SENSITIVE
MATERIAL Be careful of any language regarding sexual orientation that
may be read as derogatory or offensive by an audition panel. Consider
whether strong expletives or overtly sexual content may upset your audience. Ask yourself, "Could this material really offend someone?"

BE MINDFUL OF HOW YOU SHOW YOURSELF. Beware of typecast-
ing yourself. If you do a monologue about what it is like to be a gay man, it
may be wonderful, but may lead people to think of you first and foremost as
a gay man. If you do a monologue about being a fat girl, that's what the auditioners will think of when they think of you. Make sure that your chosen

material allows people to see the casting possibilities you want to feature, and not just one, narrow aspect of yourself.

DON'T USE SCREENPLAYS OR TV SHOW SCRIPTS. It is just too risky that people will know them and expect you to be someone other than who you are.

ALSO, BE CAREFUL WHEN EXCERPTING MONOLOGUES FROM NOVELS. It seems like a great idea, but I have yet to see one that works.

DO FIND A MONOLOGUE WHERE YOU CAN NOT ONLY CONNECT TO THE CHARACTER, BUT THROUGH THE CHARACTER CAN COMMUNICATE TO YOUR AUDIENCE AND TOUCH THEM OR AFFECT THEM IN SOME WAY.

Q: *How important is it to go to a big name school?*
A: It depends. When we are talking about a "big name school" we are talking about training programs like Yale and NYU (and others) —the programs that most aspiring actors apply to. You are bound to get top-notch training at one of these top-notch schools, but please keep this in mind: being admitted to and attending a top program is not the only way to train as an actor and make a career as an actor, and plenty of actors who attend even these wonderful programs still struggle. It is not like being accepted into a top program is an admission into the "acting club." While having these schools on your resume will certainly make the industry take your craft more seriously, it is not the only way, nor is it a guarantee of an acting career. Also, keep in mind that there are some wonderful programs out there that do not have big names. Do not feel like your life as an actor is over if you don't get into one of these big name programs. There are plenty of avenues to be explored. Wait for the right fit. The best training program is the one that is right for you and the one that is excited about training you.

Q: *In addition to monologues, some schools ask for singing as well in the audition. Why do they ask for this? I don't have any experience as a singer.*

A: Over the years, more and more schools have asked actors to sing at their auditions. There may or may not be a singing component to their training. Singing is a very good way for an audition panel to quickly assess the actor's instrument and sense of rhythm. In my experience, an actor who can sing often understands Shakespeare and other heightened text work more easily. An actor with a sense of rhythm as a singer often has comedic timing. Singing is a good way to get a better feel for the actor, but is by no means the final word or only way to understand an actor's capabilities.

If you don't sing, don't worry! Many times in program auditions singing is optional. If it is optional, only sing if you think that you're good at it. If it is required, pick something very, very musically simple where you can use the song to show your acting ability. Actor Elaine Stritch can only sing five notes in her old age, but wow can she sell a song as an actor. If you know nothing about singing, hire a coach or a music student who need some cash. Have them help you find a simple piece that you can do with confidence.

Q: *If a school interviews me at the audition, how do I prepare? What kinds of questions might they ask?*

A: Sometimes after you audition for a training program, the auditioners will have a brief chat with you. This may indicate their specific interest in you, or it may be a courtesy that they extend to all auditioning actors; it depends on the school. The best thing that you can do to prepare for this is to read the program's website to understand as much as you can about the training that they offer. The more that you understand their specific program, the more on top of it you look.

The biggest questions such schools usually ask is "Why do you think you need more training," or "What do you hope to get out of training"? Be honest! If you think you need to work on your voice or on your body, or if you need exposure to a broader range of styles, say it. Do not think that exposing your artistic weakness is bad in this case. A training program wants to train you. If you know specifically what your weaknesses are and what you need, you appear that much more ready to benefit from the training that they have to offer. The worst answer is a generalized one. The best answer is your honest, specific take on what you need.

Q: *Who should write my recommendation letters? What if the person isn't a big name director?*

A: Have people write for you who know your acting work and your work ethic well. If you are an undergraduate student applying to graduate school or another training program, have an acting professor who knows your work well or a faculty director write for you. If you are applying to a BFA program, have a director from community theatre or a teacher from your school write for you. It not important that this person be well-known. It is more important that he or she can speak about you, your work, and your work ethic in detail. Only ask people who you know will have nice things to say about you! Enlist writers who are certain to say glowing things about you and not ambiguous things like "I cannot recommend this candidate too highly."

Q: *The school I'm applying to asked for an essay. What do I say?*

A: The short answer is "the truth." Don't try to be impressive. Don't try to list your accomplishments. Tell the truth about what you need and what you hope to accomplish through training. Give anyone reading your essay an idea of who you are. Make it short and sweet. Don't tell your whole life's story. Tell people a little bit about your challenges and your hopes and what you are looking for—and proofread it! Often the reason schools ask for essays is not really to hear your reasons for wanting training, but to take a look at your written communication skills. This is especially true for programs where there is a written thesis component. An admissions committee needs to know that the student actor can handle the scholarship aspect of training. So what you say may not be as important as how you say it.

Q: *The school that I was accepted to doesn't have a showcase. How important is a showcase?*

A: A showcase is just what it sounds like. At the end of training, many programs (both BFA and MFA) will have an afternoon or evening of mini-performances intended for agents and managers to see. It is designed to show all members of the graduating class equally and to show off each person's type and strengths as performers.

Many actors think that a showcase is the be-all and end-all of their training experience. It is not. It is simply a capstone and just one of many brushes with the industry that you will have in your career. A showcase is a nice way to be seen by agents and other professionals, but it is not the only way to be seen. Even if you are seen by industry and industry expresses interest in you, it does not necessarily mean that you will form a lasting alliance. I have known many actors who had a great deal of interest paid to them at showcases that waned very shortly afterward. If your program offers a showcase, that's great! Use it to show yourself as favorably as possible. If your training program does not offer a showcase, do not worry. It is only one of many ways to be seen.

Q: *I want to go to graduate school in acting, but I did not major in acting as an undergrad. Can I still do it?*

A: Yes. Your author here was an English literature major in undergrad and went on to graduate school in theatre and a career teaching acting. It really depends on the criteria of the particular program that you are applying to. Many programs are enlightened enough to know that there are many paths to becoming an actor. An undergraduate education in acting is only one path.

Q: *I want to get my MFA in acting. What if I don't get into the program that I want right away?*

A: It happens all the time. Getting into training programs is competitive, and getting into the better ones is tough. If you do not get into the program of your dreams right away, take time off, work, save money, continue to develop your skills as an actor, and try again the following year. Look at your audition material again the next time around. Could your material be stronger or fresher? Most of the actors I know who went to top training programs did not get in right away. It took them two or three tries. Not getting into your dream school can feel crushing in the moment. It does not mean that it won't happen. It may just mean that you are not ready for them or they are not ready for you—or it may mean that there is some place that is even more right for you than your dream school.

Do not give up! If you want it, it will happen. It may not look exactly the way you think it should look—it may not be the school that you hoped for at the time that you hoped for it—but it will happen. Had I got into my dream school at the time that I wanted to go there, I would not have the career I have today. My journey required patience, strategizing, better audition material, and a little more life experience before the right place found me and I found it. Yours may, too. You may be one of the lucky ones who makes it work right out of the starting gate, or you might be like me and many, many of my very gifted students and colleagues. Have patience, work hard, and know that there is a plan for you. There was for me.

Resources

Here are some great resources that will give you more information about auditioning:

- *Audition*, by Michael Shurtleff (this is not only a wonderful audition guide, but a great brief textbook on the craft of acting)
- *Auditioning: An Actor-Friendly Guide*, by Joanna Merlin and Harold Prince (a good, general-purpose auditioning "how to" book with a different perspective than the Shurtleff book)
- *The Monologue Audition: A Practical Guide for Actors*,

by Karen Kohlhaas (a craft book: ways of approaching a monologue from a text analysis standpoint)
- *The Complete Professional Audition*, by Darren Cohen (recommended for those seeking careers in musical theatre as well as straight acting)

And these are some terrific books about the business side of acting:

- *How to Be a Working Actor*, by Mari Henry and Lynne Rogers (a great general-purpose business book for actors)
- *Acting: Make It Your Business*, by Paul Russell (a good career guide for those who think they need to become a little more business-savvy)
- *Acting as a Business, Third Edition: Strategies for Success*, by Brian O'Neil (especially recommended for those actors who are interested in stage careers in the New York market)

§

Professor Laura Wayth is available for audition coaching via Skype.

She can be contacted at San Francisco State University at lwayth@sfsu.edu. Please include the subject line: Coaching.

bibliography

The Academy Literature and Drama Website. "Jacques Lecoq 1921–1999."
  http://dlibrary.acu.edu.au/staffhome/siryan/academy
  /theatres/..%5Ctheatres%5Clecoq,%20jacques.htm.

———. "Jerzy Grotowski 1933–1999." http://dlibrary.acu.edu.au
  /staffhome/siryan/academy/theatres/..%5Ctheatres%5Cgrotowski,%20
  jerzy.htm.

———. "Tadashi Suzuki 1939–." http://dlibrary.acu.edu.au/staffhome
  /siryan/academy/theatres/..%5Ctheatres%5Csuzuki,%20t.htm.

———. "V. E. Meyerhold 1873–1940." http://dlibrary.acu.edu.au
  /staffhome/siryan/academy/theatres/..%5Ctheatres%5Cmeyerho
  ld,%20v.htm.

Adams, Cindy. 1980. *Lee Strasberg: The Imperfect Genius of the Actors
  Studio.* New York: Doubleday.

Alexander Technique Nebraska and Toronto. "The Complete Guide to
  the Alexander Technique." www.alexandertechnique.com.

Bartow, Arthur. 2006. *Training of the American Actor.* New York:
  Theatre Communications Group.

Beginners Guide to Acting. 2012–2013. "Acting Methods."
  www.beginnersguidetoacting.com/acting-methods.html.

Benedetti, Jean. 2005. *Stanislavski: An Introduction.* New York: Theatre
  Arts, Routledge.

233

Blair, Rhonda, ed. 2010. *Acting: The First Six Lessons, Documents from the American Lab Theatre*. London and New York: Routledge.

Bogart, Anne. 1995. *Viewpoints*. Ed. Michael Dixon and Joel A. Smith. Lyme, NH: Smith and Kraus.

Bogart, Anne, and Tina Landau. 2005. *The Viewpoints Book: A Practical Guide to Viewpoints and Composition*. New York: Theatre Communications Group.

Borny, Geoffrey. 2006. *Interpreting Chekhov*. Canberra, Australia: ANU E Press.

Bruder, Cohn, et al. 1986. *A Practical Handbook for the Actor*. New York: Random House.

Brustein, Robert. 1967. *Seasons of Discontent*. New York: Simon and Shuster.

Budraitis, Paul. 2012. "A Blood Test—The Actor Training Method of Tadashi Suzuki."

Degenerate Art Stream, September 19. http://degenerateartstream.blogspot .com/2012/09/tadashi-suzuki-is-theatre-director-and.html

Chekhov, Michael. 1985. *Lessons for the Professional Actor*. New York: PAJ Books.

———. 1991. *On the Technique of Acting*. New York: Harper Perennial.

Clurman, Harold. 1957. *The Fervent Years*. New York: Hill and Wang.

Cohen, Lola, ed. 2010. *The Lee Strasberg Notes*. London and New York: Routledge.

Connected Movement. "Laban Movement Analysis." http:// connectedmovement.com/Laban%20Movement%20Analysis.html.

Dalton, Lisa. 2008. "The Psychological Gesture: Hollywood's Best Kept Acting Secret!" *Actors Ink* 35 and 36. www.michaelchekhov.net /gesture.html.

Daly, Owen. "Statement of Principles—Jerzy Grotowski." owendaly.com /jeff/grotows2.htm.

Epictetus. 2011. *The Enchiridion*. Trans. Elizabeth Carter. Amazon Digital Services. Kindle e-book.

Farrell, Brian. 2010. "Nothing Else Seems to Matter." April 25.
www.brianfarrell.ca/nothing-else-seems-to-matter.

Frome, Shelly. 2001. *The Actors Studio: A History*. Jefferson, NC:
McFarland & Company.

Garfield, David. 1980. *A Player's Place*. New York: Macmillan Publishing.

Goto, Yukihiro. 1989. "The Theatrical Fusion of Suzuki Tadashi." *Asian
Theatre Journal* 6 (2): 103–123.

Grotowski, Jerzy. 1968. *Towards a Poor Theatre*. New York: Simon &
Schuster.

Hagen, Uta. 1991. *A Challenge for the Actor*. New York: Scribner.

Hardcastle, Terry. 2013. *Considering Strasberg's Method in the Twenty
-First Century: A New Pedagogy*. VCU Digital Archives. Virginia
Commonwealth University, May 9. http://hdl.handle.net/ 10156/4176.

Hirsh, Foster. 1984. *A Method to Their Madness*. New York: W. W. Norton
& Company.

Horwitz, Simi. 2001. "Tadashi Suzuki" [sic]. *Backstage*, November 14.
www.backstage.com/news/tadashi-sazuki-seeking-a-common
-grammar.

Hull, S. Lorraine. 1985. *Strasberg's Method as Taught by Lorrie Hull*.
Woodbridge: Ox Bow Publishing.

Jason Bennett Actor's Workshop. "Jerzy Grotowski." www.jbactors.com
/actingreading/actingteacherbiographies/jerzygrotowski.html.

———. "Uta Hagen." www.jbactors.com/actingreading
actingteacherbiographics/utahagen.html.

Kazan, Elia. 1988. *Elia Kazan: A Life*. New York: Knopf.

Krebs, Nancy. "What Is Lessac Kinesensic Training?" The Voiceworks.
www.nancykrebs.com/lessac-kinesensic-training.php.

Mamet, David. 1994. *4 a.m.—A Short Play*. In *Goldberg Street: Short
Plays and Monologues by David Mamet*. New York: Grove.

Meisner, Sanford. 1987. *On Acting*. New York: Random House.

Merlin, Bella. 2007. *The Complete Stanislavsky Toolkit*. Hollywood, CA:
Quite Specific Media Group, Ltd.

Mestnik, Elizabeth. 2011. "What Does the Meisner Technique Teach?" *EmasLA Blog*, June 16. www.emasla.com/blog/2011/06/16/what-does -the-meisner-technique-teach.

———. 2011. "Beyond Repetition." *EmasLA Blog*, June 21. www.emasla.com/blog/2011/06/21/beyond-repetition-%E2%80%93 -by-elizabeth-mestnik.

Moffit, D. E. "Viola Spolin." www.spolin.com/violabio.

Moore, Sonia. 1965. "The Method of Physical Actions." *The Tulane Drama Review* 9 (4): 91–94.

———. 1984. *The Stanislavski System*. Middlesex, England: Penguin Books.

National Michael Chekhov Association. 1986. "Who Is Michael Chekhov?" www.chekhov.net/chekhovintro.html.

NSW HSC Online. "Approaches to Acting: Study Guide Jacques Lecoq." www.hsc.csu.edu.au/drama/hsc/studies/topics/3265/lecoq.htm.

———. "Overview of Meyerhold's *Approach to Acting*." www.hsc.csu.edu.au/drama/hsc/studies/topics/3265/Meyerhold /overview.htm.

Oxley, Natasha. 2006. "Getting to Grips with Grotowski." www.kent.ac.uk/arts/research/Grotowski/GROTOWSKIESSAY.pdf.

Overlie, Mary. "The Project: The Beginning of the Theory." Six Viewpoints: A Deconstructive Approach to Theater. http://sixviewpoints.com/Theory_1.html.

Petit, Lenard. 2009. *The Michael Chekhov Handbook for the Actor*. New York: Routledge.

Pugatch, Jason. 2006. *Acting Is a Job: Real Life Lessons about the Acting Business*. New York: Allworth Press.

Robinson, Alice M., Vera Mowry Roberts, and Mily S. Barranger, ed. 1989. *Notable Women in the American Theatre: A Biographical Dictionary*. Westport, CT: Greenwood Press.

Rotté, Joanna. 2000. *Acting with Adler*. New York: Proscenium Publishers, Inc.

Schwartz, Gary. 2012a. "The Difference between Spolin Games and Popular Improv." Improv Odyssey, November 13. www.improv-odyssey.com/the-difference-between-spolin-games-and -popular-improv/.

———. 2012b. "What's in a Game?" Intuitive Learning Systems, May. www.spolin.com/whats-in-a-game-2/.

Spolin, Viola. 1999. *Improvisation for the Theater*. Evanston, IL: Northwestern University Press.

Strasberg, Lee. 1988. *A Dream of Passion*. New York: Penguin.

Vocal Yoga. "Fitzmaurice Voicework." http://vocalyoga.com /fitzmaurice-voicework.

Westbrook, Mark. 2008. "Practical Aesthetics—An Overview." EzineArticles, August 8. http://ezinearticles.com /?Practical-Aesthetics---An-Overview&id=1395198.

———. 2010. "Method Acting and Practical Aesthetics: What's The Difference?" Acting Coach Scotland, August 10. http://actingcoachscotland.co.uk/2010/08/method-acting-and -practical-aesthetics-whats-the-difference.

index